I0087259

THINK CHRISTMAS

THINK
CHRISTMAS

A STUDY OF THE INCARNATION FROM
PHILIPPIANS 2:1–11

STEPHEN MANLEY

CROSS
STYLE
PRESS

THINK CHRISTMAS
A Study of the Incarnation from Philippians 2:1–11

© 2024 by Stephen Manley

Published by Cross Style Press
Lebanon, Tennessee
CrossStyle.org

All rights reserved. No part of this book may be reproduced in any form without prior permission from the publisher, except for brief quotations.

Scripture quotations are from The ESV® Bible (The Holy Bible, English Standard Version®), © 2001 by Crossway, a publishing ministry of Good News Publishers. Used by permission. All rights reserved.

ISBN (Print): 978-1-957219-04-2
ISBN (eBook): 978-1-957219-03-5

Printed in the United States of America.

CrossStyle.org

CONTENTS

1

THINK CHRISTMAS

Philippians 2:1-11

"So if there is any encouragement in Christ, any comfort from love, any participation in the Spirit, any affection and sympathy, complete my joy by being of the same mind. having the same love, being in full accord and of one mind. Do nothing from selfish ambition or conceit, but in humility count others more significant than yourselves. Let each of you look not only to his own interests, but also to the interests of others. Have this mind among yourselves, which is yours in Christ Jesus, who, though He was in the form of God, did not count equality with God a thing to be grasped, but emptied Himself, by taking the form of a servant, being born in the likeness of men. And being found in human form, He humbled Himself by becoming obedient to the point of death, even death on a cross. Therefore God has highly exalted Him and bestowed on Him the name that is above every name, so that at the name of Jesus every knee should bow, in heaven and on earth

and under the earth, and every tongue confess that Jesus Christ is Lord, to the glory of God the Father" (Philippians 2:1-11).

Even the secular world embraces, to some degree, the mindset of the Christmas season. Christmas is about joy, family, love, being together, generosity, and giving! The commercial world has captured this perspective; Christmas is the highest sales period of the entire year. Some stores support their whole year just on the Christmas sales. We go into debt; we buy foolish things, all because we are driven by this desire to give. Parents feel terrible when they cannot provide their children with all the toys and gimmicks they want.

Where did this come from in the secular world? This feeling and desire to give came from the Christian movement. Suddenly, the sky is split open, and an angelic host echoes the message of the angel to the shepherds:

"Glory to God in the highest, and on earth peace among those with whom He is pleased" (Luke 2:14)!

The message is God gives a great gift to humanity! It is time to rejoice; celebration is in order! It is an excellent occasion for generosity beyond compare!

Wisemen traveled from the East for two years at great sacrifice. They invested their time and money, leaving their families behind. Following the star, they arrived in Bethlehem, where Jesus was living. Trembling, they approached the house to fall down and worship Him. *"Then, opening their treasures, they offered Him gifts, gold and frankincense and myrrh"* (Matthew 2:11). Did they buy something? What did they receive in return? It was not about "getting" but about "giving." It is the spirit of Christmas! This spirit dominated the Christian experience and influenced the world. While the world has perverted the spirit of giving, the basic principle behind the spirit still belongs to God!

Here is what is remarkable about this focus! The spirit of Christmas is the Spirit of Jesus! We can trace every generous thought at Christmas back to Jesus. But notice Paul links the Christmas event of Christ's coming to His crucifixion. *"And being found in human form, He humbled Himself by becoming obedient to the point of death, even death on a cross"* (Philippians 2:8). In spirit, Christmas and Good Friday are one event! The mindset of Christmas is the mindset of Jesus' crucifixion. To embrace Christmas is to embrace the crucifixion event! The spirit of Christmas giving was not isolated to the beginning of Christ's life but flowed throughout and erupted clearly in the end.

Paul divided the passages' structure into two parts, describing an attitude. But it was not an attitude determined by life's circumstances or outside influence. A deep inner Spirit, at the core of a person's existence, masters the individual's perspective. In the first four verses, Paul describes this attitude or Spirit! Then he breaks into a hymn (Philippians 2:5-11). The early Church quoted and sang this hymn again and again. It was at the heart of their pronouncement of the Gospel message. The incarnation and crucifixion intertwine into one declaration. They were declaring one spirit, attitude!

Paul begins by listing attributes connected to this attitude (Philippians 2:1-4). *"Encouragement in Christ"* is the beginning. The Greek word "paraklesis" means "consolation, exhortation, admonition, or encouragement to strengthen and establish the believer in the faith." The same basic Greek word is used for *"Helper"* (parakletos) as Jesus refers to the Holy Spirit (John 14:16, 26; 15:26). Paul continues with *"comfort from love"* (Philippians 2:1). While both words express the same attitude, they are different. *"Comfort from love"* (paramythion) indicates the resource used by the comforting one. *"Encouragement"* (paraklesis) stresses the process or progress of the act. Paul describes a consistent flow of the attitude of encouragement through the instrument of love within the individual.

Paul declares a *"participation* (koinonia) *in the Spirit,"* a business term regarding partnership, describing the source of the attitude in the merger with the Spirit of Jesus. He quickly moves to the location of this merger and attitude. *"Affection"* (splagchnon) relates to the body's intestines. The deep inner gut of a person is merged with the Spirit to flow the attitude of encouragement, the same description of Jesus, who *"had compassion"* when He saw the multitudes (Matthew 9:36). *"Mercy"*(oiktirmos) is the pity or compassion that one shows for the sufferings of others.

Paul challenges everyone to embrace this attitude (Philippians 2:2) but quickly returns to the description. This essential attitude has *"no selfish ambition"* (eritheian). This word relates to being hired for a job. One does not care about the job but only what they will get. It is working only for self-interest. Paul links this with *"conceit"* (kenodoxian), which focuses on pride and doing only for self-praise. While this is the negative approach, he quickly turns to the positive, *"lowliness of mind"* (tapeinophrosyne), a description of humility, esteeming yourself less than others. He duplicates this statement by crying, **"Count others more significant than yourselves"** (hegeomai). This Greek word has to do with being first or being a leader. We are to lead the way in considering others more significant than ourselves. We must not merely *"look not only"* (skopeite) for our interest, **"but also for the interest of others"** (Philippians 2:4). This means "to spy out, look towards an object, to contemplate, give attention!"

PERSPECTIVE

Is this not a description of the deep-seated attitude of Jesus at Christmas? Is this not the Christmas spirit? Is this not the deep-seated attitude of the cross? Is this not the crucifixion spirit? This perspective includes the mindset, way of thinking, attitude, opinion, and basic premise of His birth, life, and death! Paul proposes a merger with His Spirit until we also experience His mindset. *"Let this mind be in you which was also in Christ Jesus"* (Philippians 2:5).

This premise is so rooted in the New Testament that we titled it "cross style." We named our ministry after this principle. The cross style is to be the attitude in every function of ministry and life. No one can live for themselves and be a Kingdom person. The birth and death of Jesus strikes a blow at the very core of sin, self-centeredness. Every sinful deed flows from the nature of sin, self-centeredness. When self-centeredness is in a deed, that deed immediately becomes destructive and sinful. Religious, criminal, and good deeds are all sinful when self-centeredness is responsible for the action.

The activity of any deed cannot define sin. We must consistently recognize the nature of its cause. Jesus died not to save us from wrong deeds but from the sinful nature. Christianity is not a reformation of acts but a transformation of the mind! *"Do not be conformed to this world, but be transformed by the renewal of your mind, that by testing you may discern what is the will of God, what is good and acceptable and perfect"* (Romans 12:2). While we must understand our actions will change, activity is not the focus. Any attempt to alter the activity without changing nature increases pride and self-centeredness. It defeats the purpose of the change.

The mindset of Christ is "bleed, suffer, and die." The perspective of "never think about yourself" is its core. When was this not the expression of Jesus? Christmas is the story of One *"who, though He was in the form of God, did not count equality with God a thing to be grasped"* because He was God (Philippians 2:6). However, Jesus assumed *"the form of a bondservant, and coming in the likeness of men"* becoming one with us (Philippians 2:7). Is this not cross style? *"He humbled Himself and became obedient to the point of death, even the death of a cross"* (Philippians 2:8). Is not the cross a prime example of cross style? We see the constant demonstration of such a style between His birth and His death. From washing the disciples' feet (John 13:1-17) to healing a centurion's son (Matthew 8:5-13), Jesus lived the style of the cross. It is an expression of who He is!

PASSIVE

The cross style is the challenge of Christianity. I am to be Christlike! While I may be able to express some generosity towards others during Christmas, the problem is the rest of the year and expressing this towards everyone. There are a select few to whom I may express the cross-style attitude, and they are limited in number. The ability to extend forgiveness to everyone while dying on a cross just is not in my nature. Is this mindset something I must learn, develop, or master? Do I need more training in this area? Are there books to read and seminars to attend that will aid me in mastering such a lifestyle?

Paul said, *"Have this mind among yourselves, which is yours in Christ Jesus"* (Philippians 2:5). It would aid us to examine the translation of this Greek text. The second Greek word in the text is "gar," not translated in most translations. It is usually translated as "for," which proposes the reason for the previous statements. What Paul proposes in the first four verses is based on the nature of Jesus expressed in Christmas and the crucifixion. This attitude or nature is in Jesus! Can we find it anywhere outside of Jesus? While many people have sacrificed for others, is there anyone in the history of the world who adequately expressed this mindset outside of Jesus?

The cross style is the startling premise of Christianity. It is impossible! Within the boundaries of Christlikeness, we constantly struggle to maintain the radical high standard of Jesus. We continually dumb down the standard of Christianity for the sake of convenience and attainability. We do precisely what the Pharisees did in the Old Testament. We argue over which is the greatest commandment because we cannot keep them all. We establish acceptable activities that give us a sense of accomplishment regarding the cross style. That was the great concern about calling any ministry "cross style" for fear we would develop a series of laws or activities. "Bleed, suffer, and die," and "never think about yourself" can never be just an activity. It is a nature!

The third word in the Greek text is "phroneistho." "Phroneistho" presents the statement's main verb and subject. It is an imperative verb, which gives the assumed subject of "you," meaning to dispose of your mind in a certain way. Paul relates this to the perspective *"in Christ Jesus."* Incredibly, the voice of this verb is "passive!" That means the subject is not responsible for the verb's action; something or someone beyond yourself is acting upon "you." "You" are commanded to "allow" or *"Let"* the "thought process" of Jesus dominate your life, not a command to "do," but to "submit" to the influence of this mindset of Jesus. Do not misunderstand; there is radical activity involved. However, Paul does not highlight the details of the action, which is the nature of the mindset. Christmas and crucifixion are the radical activities displaying this mindset in Jesus. No one proposes those same extreme activities for our lives. However, when we are under the influence of this mindset, others will see the same radical expressions in the necessary actions of our lives.

Paul expresses the same reality, *"In Christ Jesus!"* *"In"* is an expression of "abiding" or "fixed." In all his epistles, Paul makes us aware we only find the resources "in" Jesus. The Trinity God *"has blessed us in Christ with every spiritual blessing in the heavenly places"* (Ephesians 1:3).

"The heavenly places" relate to the spiritual realm, not to the final destination of the believer. In the mystical, unseen, spiritual world, Jesus can unite with me. His nature and my nature merge, forming a new creature. His nature can invade my nature until the mindset of His being becomes mine. He wants to act upon the nature of my life, demonstrating His cross style thinking in my world.

In his early days, Martin Luther desired the righteousness of Christ. He made a list of activities upon which to focus to experience such. Each day, Martin checked his list and found he fell short of this righteousness. But one particular day, great excitement gripped him. He had accomplished the list perfectly. As he boasted about his accomplishment, he realized the greatest of all sins had overcome him: pride! This mindset can never be of us; it is only *"in Christ Jesus!"* He must invade our lives with His thinking.

PERMANENT

God never intended this attitude of *"consolation in Christ," "comfort of love," "affection and mercy,"* and *"lowliness of mind."* God never intended this attitude to be experienced only during the Christmas season. This mindset is the constant expression of the Christian! There is to be no wavering in its perspective. The cross style is the style of the nature of the new creature. Again, this presents an impossibility for the new creature to produce through the self-centeredness of humanity. The act of such a self-production only creates more self-centeredness. This attitude is experienced within the human being as one merges with Jesus!

Paul's statement expresses this consistency. ***"Have this mind among yourselves, which is yours in Christ Jesus"*** (Philippians 2:5). You will notice Paul states ***"in"*** twice, relating both to the Christian and Jesus! "Into" is a translation of the Greek word "eis," which is a movement term; "from" is a translation of the Greek word "ek" or "apo," which is a movement term. But ***"in,"*** translated from "en," eliminates movement; it is fixed, expressing abiding or remaining. This nature expressed in this mindset is a permanent, fixed, or abiding reality in Jesus. There was never a time when He did not demonstrate "the bleed, suffer, and die" lifestyle. Jesus never thought about Himself! Now, this exact nature is ***"in"*** us ***"in"*** the same way it was ***"in"*** Him!

Paul again expresses the merger of our nature and Jesus' nature in the new creature. We are ***"in Christ Jesus."*** The Holy Spirit, the nature of Jesus, dwells in us. He is expressing His lifestyle through us. We now experience what is impossible for us through His presence. This lifestyle fulfills the Law and the Prophets (Matthew 5:17). The carnal person, filled with himself, cannot keep the Old Covenant. But the wonder of the New Covenant is ***"in Christ Jesus."*** All that He is now dwells in us, and we dwell in Him. Jesus' nature and our nature have merged, expressing His nature.

The main verb of Paul's statement validates this truth. The Greek word "phroneistho" is translated as ***"Have this mind"*** (Philippians 2:5). It is an imperative meaning a command and is in the present tense. In this verb tense, the writer portrays an act in process or a state of being with no assessment of the action's completion. This attitude is to be in the present with continual action into the future.

16

There is no prediction of when we should not express this attitude. This spontaneous eruption of "bleed, suffer, and die" and "never think about yourself" spills from the nature of Jesus, indwelling the believer. The secret is not in the effort, attempt, or struggle of the believer but in the yielding, abandonment, and submission of the believer to Jesus. There is no highlight on the believer, but we see Jesus through the believer!

2

THE CONTRAST

Philippians 2:6

"Who, though He was in the form of God, did not count it equality with God a thing to be grasped" *(Philippians 2:6).*

Paul's overall purpose in our passage is to establish a blaring contrast between the spirit of Christmas and the spirit of Halloween (Philippians 2:1-11). He does so in the first four verses. In the second section, he illustrates it in Jesus (Philippians 2:5-11)! Paul characterizes the spirit of Christmas as **"affection and mercy"** (Philippians 2:1). This spirit flows from deep in the internal core of the individual as other's needs move them. The **"comfort of love"** is the resource flowing into **"encouragement"** to adequately strengthen and enable the person in need. It is the spirit of "bleed, suffer, and die" and "never think about yourself!"

Paul urges the Christians of Philippi to embrace this spirit. Does this spirit exist in Christ Jesus? Is it not the very heart of God's nature, demonstrating itself in His

Christmas gift to you? *"For God so loved the world, that He gave His only Son, that whoever believes in Him should not perish but have eternal life"* (John 3:16). *"In this the love of God was made manifest among us, that God sent His only Son into the world, so that we might live through Him. In this is the love, not that we have loved God but that He loved us and sent His Son to be the propitiation for our sins"* (1 John 4:9-10). Could I not quote the entire New Testament as validation of this one fact? Jesus is the *"comfort of love"* flowing from the deepest core of God, *"affection,"* because our need moves Him, *"mercy."* This resource would not allow Him to sit on the sideline and watch our struggle. Still, He became the *"encouragement"* of our redemption and entered into our suffering! Jesus is the giving Spirit of Christmas!

The spirit of Christmas is opposite the spirit of Halloween. If you do not give to me, I will trick you. The founder of the Church of Satan in America, Anton Lavey, who is now dead, stated, "I am glad that Christian parents allow their children to worship the devil at least one night out of the year." Anyone connected with spiritual warfare understands Halloween as a demonic holiday. The spirit of Halloween is "You must give to me, or I will trick you." While the costume may not be a devil or witch, the attitude is the same. I don't want to enter into a debate about Halloween only to offer it as an example that contrasts with the Christmas spirit. The demonic spirit is not one of giving but one of getting. This spirit does not express the "bleed, suffer, and die" and "never think about yourself." Its expression is "grab, get, and protect" and "always think about yourself." Paul describes it in his contrast as *"selfish ambition or conceit"* (Philippians 2:3). While one might argue that the spirit of Christmas has become what many, and certainly our children, expect to receive from Santa Claus, this only illustrates how strong the demonic force is to pervert the spirit of Christmas. But all Christians know it is a perversion of the real Spirit of Christmas.

Throughout all of Paul's epistles, he contrasts these two spirits. He admonishes us to *"Walk in the Spirit"* (Galatians 5:16). How would such be manifested? *"But the fruit of the Spirit is love, joy, peace, patience, kindness, goodness, faithfulness, gentleness, self-control; against such there is no law"* (Galatians 5:22-23). But what are the works of the demonic spirit? *"Sexual immorality, impurity, sensuality, idolatry, sorcery, enmity, strife, jealousy, fits of anger, rivalries, dissensions, divisions, envy, drunkenness, orgies, and things like these. I warn you, as I warned you before, that those who do such things will not inherit the kingdom of God"* (Galatians 5:19-21). All of the *"such things"* are characterized by selfish desires. Notice the immensity of the list connected to the demonic spirit and the preciseness of the list of the Spirit of Christmas.

However, Paul gives little time to the demonic spirit in our Philippians passage. We are not confused about the selfish, live-for-yourself spirit that has possessed human life. We have all experienced its depth and have expressed it in our own way. But Paul goes overboard to give the most outstanding example, displaying the most excellent quality of the spirit of Christmas. He expands it into Good Friday, the crucifixion! This Spirit is Jesus! He is going to expound, not on the physical appearance of the spirit of Christmas, but will expose the depth of what this spirit looks like in the heart of God!

Jesus, *"Who, though He was in the form of God, did not count equality with God a thing to be grasped"* (Philippians 2:6). The Greek word translated as *"though He was"* is "hyparcho." It combines the Greek words "hupo" and "archo." "Hupo" presents an emphasis on "under or through," while "archo" means "to begin." Together, they proclaim "to be or exist in a state or condition that is most often a state that endures as opposed to one that is temporary." When this Greek word is combined with a prepositional phrase such as *"in the form of God,"* and the phrase contains a dative such as *"form,"* it implies a being, remaining, or living in a state or place.

Paul declares that Jesus dwells in a state of being that involves permanency. Jesus *"was in the form of God,"* which was not temporary, something He finally achieved or struggled to accomplish. *"Was in the form of God"* is simply who He is, who He was, and who He will be. It is the state of His existence, further verified by the present tense verb "hyparcho!" Paul portrays a state of being with no assessment of the state coming to an end. It is essential to note that Jesus has always been God and never gave up this state of existence. One must never say that Jesus gave up being God to become man. He did NOT! That is why we consistently refer to Jesus as God-Man! In the incarnation, the spirit of Christmas, Jesus assumed the nature and body of humanity so that in one person, there was God's and man's total nature in an indissoluble union. Any degrading of His position as God undermined the redemptive power of His death!

This state of being was *"in the form of God."* The Greek word translated as *"form"* is "morphe." While God is Spirit, and we cannot see Him, Paul understood He existed in a *"form"* or shape. God is not a concept invented by needy humanity but, in reality, does not exist. He is not an influence or force in the universe but has no *"form."* The very idea of *"form"* presumes an objective reality. No one who is not God could be in the *"form"* of God! The same person of God in the Old Testament, assuming the shape of *"pillar of cloud"* and *"pillar of fire,"* was the objective reality of God (Exodus 13:21, 22). While God is Spirit, He consistently reveals Himself as a Person. He expresses the three essential elements of personality: mind, will, and emotion. Jesus is eternally this God person!

To verify that Jesus is *"in the form of God,"* Paul declares that Jesus *"did not count equality with God a thing to be grasped."* The Greek word "hegesato" is translated as *"did consider."* It is in the indicative mood, which presents it as a solid statement of fact. It is "to lead out before the mind," thus "to view, regard, esteem, count, or reckon." Since Jesus is God in objective reality, He did not give it a second thought to actively engage in all the attitudes, attributes, and advantages of being God. As I rise in the morning and without thinking, I assume all that is involved in being human, so Jesus, without thinking, assumes all involved in being God! I never worry about waking up and not being human; I do not struggle to be human; I am naturally engaged in all the struggles involved. Jesus operates without effort within the boundaries of being God, for He is God!

It never entered Jesus's thinking that it was *"equality with God a thing to be grasped."* The Greek word "harpagmon" is translated as *"grasped."* It means "to seize upon with force," and our passage is the only place in the New Testament where this Greek word appears.

The Holy Spirit isolated "harpagmon" for its exclusive use regarding the opposite of what Jesus experienced as God. The objective reality of Jesus being in the form of God could not render His claim of equality with God as robbery. Jesus did not esteem being equal with God as identical with the coming forth or action of a robbery. There is nothing suspicious, skeptical, or uncertain about Jesus being God. Let it be, now and forever, understood and accepted in our reality that Jesus is God!

We must further understand Jesus is not "almost God," "nearly God," or "merely a part of God." Paul uses the words *"equality with God."* The Greek word "eimi" is translated as *"to be."* It is an infinitive verb that gives reason to the previous statement. Why did Jesus not consider it robbery? He has *"equality with God."* "Eimi" is a state of being, not an activity. Again, this verifies the *"equality"* statement Paul already made. Jesus is in a state of existence as God. The Greek word translated as *"equal"* is "isos." It refers to having the same quality, quantity, value, or measure of another. There is no robbery or deception involved in proclaiming that Jesus is God. "Who He is" and "Who God is" are the same!

While Jesus did not give up who He is, He did give up the advantages of who He is. Jesus surrendered all the benefits of being God to assume flesh and redeem humanity. God is eternal and beyond death. If the *"wages of sin is death,"* how is God going to redeem humanity (Romans 6:23). God is incapable of dying on the cross and assuming our sin. But Jesus, who is God, gave up every advantage of being God and became man! Jesus *"emptied Himself, by taking the form of a servant, being born in the likeness of men. And being found in human form,*

He humbled Himself by becoming obedient to the point of death, even the death on a cross" (Philippians 2:7-8). Jesus obedience is the spirit of Christmas. It is a "bleed, suffer, and die" and "never think about yourself" spirit! It is the heart of God, Jesus!

Paul calls us to be in Christ and assume this same spirit. If we merge with Jesus, we will think like He thinks, want what He wants, and feel like He feels. The Holy Spirit, the Spirit of Jesus, will be our spirit. Whatever is in Christ must also be in us. Paul is precise about this single fact. In Ephesians, he boldly states our position: *"And you were dead in trespasses and sin in which you once walked, following the course of this world, following the prince of the power of the air, the spirit that is now at work in the sons of disobedience - among whom we all once lived in the passions of our flesh, carrying out the desires of the body and the mind, and were by nature children of wrath, like the rest of mankind"* (Ephesians 2:1-3). The demonic nature of "grab, get, and protect" and "always think about yourself" was our nature. The spirit of Christmas was foreign to us.

Where can I find deliverance from such a nature? Regardless of how much I discipline myself, curb my desires, or have intentions of generosity, I always find selfishness dominating. It is my nature. That is Paul's cry: this nature does not exist *"in Christ!"* In Jesus, we find deliverance. Jesus does not possess "victory" and will give it to you for use apart from Him. Victory is when you are seated in the person of Jesus (Ephesians 2:6). *"In Christ,"* there is crucifixion and death to the selfish, self-centered nature, and the nature of Jesus becomes yours. There is *"encouragement in Christ," "comfort from love," "participation of the Spirit," "affection,"* and *"sympathy"* (Philippians 2:1). When you are *"in Christ,"* Jesus is in you!

Contrasting the spirit of Christmas with the demonic spirit, we discover an accurate view of sin. At the beginning of Genesis, Moses recorded the temptation and fall of man (Genesis 3). While there is a vivid picture of sin's physical involvement, the essential facts are in the spiritual realm. The serpent, trees of the garden, fruit, conversation, and eating are all a part of the activity. Still, they are only the physical stage upon which the spiritual life of humanity displays itself. The conversation between humanity and the devil is one of questioning the honesty and sovereignty of God. Did God tell us the truth? Does He have our best interest in mind? Is the spirit of Christmas His heart? Is the reality of God's expression "bleed, suffer, and die" and "never think about yourself?" The devil proposed to humanity the demonic nature of "grab, get, and protect" and "always think about yourself!"

The tragedy of that moment is not an activity but the embracing of the demonic nature. Something happened that humanity could not revoke! Instead of God filling man with the Spirit of Christmas, Satan filled humanity with the demonic nature. The distinction between these two fillings is essential. The Person, the Holy Spirit, filled Adam and Eve. This Person is the Spirit of Christmas. Due to the presence of God in their lives, the Spirit of Christmas possessed them, and they possessed the Holy Spirit. The demonic nature is not demon possession, although that can happen. The absence of God allows a person to possess himself. He becomes self-centered and self-sourced because the Holy Spirit was removed.

The devil suggested to Adam and Eve, *"For God knows that when you eat of it your eyes will be opened, and you will be like God, knowing good and evil"* (Genesis 3:5). Do you see the suggestion? All this time, humanity lived under the domination of God, was sourced by God, and had the Spirit of God. Now is the opportunity to push aside, overthrow the control of God, and source yourself! Be your own god! Yes, Adam and Eve physically expressed their disobedience, but the rebellion was much more significant than a mere physical act. Could God forgive a physical act? He is the Spirit of Christmas and could grant forgiveness, but it would not change what happened in the nature of humanity. God could have re-created the fruit on the tree and acted as if the disobedience had never happened. But humanity was not the same. The demonic nature now dominated humanity and broke the relationship with God.

Here is the amazing message of the Gospel! The Christmas spirit dwelling in the heart of God could not tolerate such a state of damnation for humanity. Remember, the Christmas spirit is "bleed, suffer, and die" and "never think about yourself." God did not get mad or seek revenge. His nature designed a way to restore and redeem humanity to its original state. Jesus, who made no effort to be God because He was God, became man! Jesus becoming man is the supreme illustration of the spirit of Christmas. We find it only in the heart of God, whose heart can now be ours!

What does that have to do with me? Adam and Eve did the wrong thing, but that was a long time ago. The reality of their physical act disrupted the spiritual world. The sons of Adam were birthed in his image and became like him in the spiritual realm (Genesis 5:3). Whatever Adam had become, he passed on to me. But it is even worse than stated, for I may blame Adam for all of my spiritual problems. However, "I thought it not robbery to be equal with humanity, but made myself of increased reputation, taking the supposed form of god, came in the appearance of being God." I have done what Adam did! I did the opposite of what Jesus did (Philippians 2:6-8). Jesus, who is God, was driven by the Christmas Spirit to give up every advantage of being God and become one with us in our humanity. He became the second Adam who refused to embrace the demonic spirit of self-sourcing and conquered sin, death, and hell. He brought an end to "grab, get, and protect" and "always think about yourself."

Paul offers us the opportunity of deliverance from our self-domination. I am my own biggest problem! My self-centeredness destroys everything good in my life and so controls me that I cannot deliver myself from myself. Jesus has come. He is my salvation. He is the Spirit of Christmas. Once again, I can live! ***"In Christ,"*** I find my actual creation!

3

EMPTIED

Philippians 2:7

"But emptied Himself, by taking the form of a servant, being born in the likeness of men" *(Philippians 2:7).*

Christmas is the physical demonstration of God's inner heart and spirit! The mind of Christ is ours in Jesus. While no one can be in Jesus without thinking like Him, so no one can think like Him without being in Jesus! His spirit is one of *"encouragement"* (paraklesis, Philippians 2:1). The focus is on the action of the resource reaching into our lives to establish and strengthen us. The resource that acts is *"any comfort from love"* (paramythion, Philippians 2:1). While "paraklesis" and "paramythion" are very similar, the "paraklesis" focuses on the activity as "paramythion" focuses on the resource. The activity of encouragement comes from the state of love existing in Jesus. The resource is located in *"affection"* (splagchnon, Philippians 2:1)) referring to the bowels of a person. This encouragement is deep within the core of Christ, creating a driving force that demands the physical demonstration of Christmas.

To illustrate this spirit in Jesus, Paul firmly establishes the deity of Christ. We only realize the wonder of the spirit of Christmas when we see His demonstration in the immensity of His sacrifice. Jesus is not one-third God, a part of God, or someone created by God. *"**Though He was in the form of God, did not count equality with God a thing to be grasped**"* (Philippians 2:6). Throughout this statement, Paul projects a "state of existence." He does not propose a theory, concept, or belief system. He makes a statement of objective reality. There is an actual Person who is God! He is not a "mother nature" figure or a mystical force of fate. He is a functioning Person with mind, will, and emotion. His name is Jesus! God's qualities, attributes, and distinctions are equally in Jesus. He is omniscience, omnipotent, and omnipresent as God. We must never refer to Jesus as less than God. He never surrendered or gave up being God. Any contact with Jesus at any time is to connect with God.

*"**BUT**"* is the opening word of our passage in the Greek text! It is not the ordinary Greek word often used for a conjunction of contrast. Instead, Paul uses the Greek word "alla" to express intensification and contrast. It is an adversative particle, originally the neuter plural of "allos," translated as "other," used to imply some diversity or superaddition to what preceded, marking opposition, antithesis, or transition. Paul just declared Jesus as God (Philippians 2:6). In his declaration, he includes "qualifying statements" to ensure the strength of the statement. Jesus is *"**in the form of God.**"* Whatever God looks like or is in His state of existence, Jesus is! He is equal with God because

He dwells in the state of being God. He did not struggle, attempt, or try to be God but was so sufficiently in the state of being God that He did not consider it *"a thing to be grasped."* Now Paul declares Jesus became human (Philippians 2:7). The contrast is so radical and extreme he uses the adversative conjunction "alla."

Paul quickly moves to "heautou," the second word in the Greek text. "Heautou" is the reflexive pronoun denoting mutual participation in an act on the part of the subject of the verb. The third Greek word is the verb "kenoo," translated as *"emptied."* This verb also contains the sentence's subject, "He," which is not translated. Therefore, a literal translation would be *"But* He *emptied Himself."* This verb is in the active voice, making the subject "He" responsible. Jesus, who is God, acted upon Himself to empty Himself! *"Emptied"* (kenoo) means to void or empty of all content, which Paul proceeds to explain.

This process included *"by taking the form of a servant."* The Greek word "lambano," translated as *"by taking,"* means to take actively. It is in the active voice (the subject is responsible for the action) and the nominative (referring to the subject "He"). Jesus is God and is responsible for *"taking."* In a previous study, we discussed "morphe," translated as *"form."* Paul used this term to refer to the state of existence in which Jesus existed as God; now, he places the same emphasis on the state of existence Jesus has as *"a servant."* Jesus is God, dwelling in a state of objective reality; Jesus is man, dwelling in a state of objective reality. However, Paul does not begin with the term "man" but *"servant"* (doulos), a person who is legally owned by another and whose entire livelihood and purpose is determined by their master.

Immediately, Paul describes this state of existence as *"being born in the likeness of men." "Being born"* is translated from the Greek word "ginomai." The primary meaning is "to begin to be, that is, to come into existence or any state." Jesus was birthed *"in the likeness of men."* The Greek word "homoioma," translated as *"likeness,"* is significant in this phrase. It means "to make like." Jesus did not choose any individual man and become him; God did not create Jesus in the image of any one person. Each of us is a unique creation in our humanity; our fingerprints, DNA, purpose, and structure are different than all other human beings. Likewise, Jesus became a man of the same uniqueness.

This verse states the doctrine of the incarnation. Incarnation means "the act of assuming flesh." This doctrine says, "The second member of the Trinity God, Jesus, left His throne to assume the body and nature of humanity. This Person consists of God's nature and the nature of humanity in an indissoluble union." The union of God and man is indissoluble, meaning no one can divide it. Jesus was not half God and half man; His manhood was not dominant sometimes, and other times, His nature as God ruled. This indissoluble union of the two natures can be described and understood in the child born of his parents. The mother cannot take her half, or the father demand his half of the child. The child is an indissoluble union of the parents!

What did it mean for Jesus to become a man? Was He a Superman? Could Jesus change from His man costume to His God reality? Was He God dressed in human flesh? Was He a fake man? Did Jesus feel like we feel? Did He need to sleep? Did Jesus get hungry? Was He attracted to girls? Did He need deodorant? How you answer these questions will determine your understanding of the Gospel. Your view of the incarnation will determine the quality of your holy lifestyle.

We do not doubt that Jesus is God; Paul firmly established this (Philippians 2:6). If Jesus is not God, there is no redemption for us. God alone can sufficiently make the sacrifice for us all. However, when He left His throne and became man, some crucial questions became relevant. As God, Jesus possesses all the attributes of God: omnipresence, omniscience, and omnipotent. But when He became a man, did He have these same qualities present in His life?

As God, Jesus is omnipresent! But as man, was He everywhere at one time? The obvious answer is no! Jesus, as a man, was limited to one space at a time, as you and I are. When He wanted to go fifteen miles from Jericho to Jerusalem, He had to walk like other humans. Jesus possessed the quality of omnipresence as God, but He *"emptied Himself"* to be human. He took His omnipresence, which is rightfully His, and set it aside to become a man. It is still His, for He is God, but He chooses not to use it to be one of us!

As God, Jesus is omniscient, knowing everything in the eternal now! But now Jesus has become a man. Does He know everything as a man? There seemed to be times when Jesus knew things an average person would not know. Yet, if there is one fact that Jesus as a Man does not know, then He is not omniscient. When Jesus spoke of His second coming, Jesus told His disciples, ***"But concerning that day or that hour no one knows, not even the angels of heaven, nor the Son, but only the***

Father" (Mark 13:32). Luke gives us the only insight we have into the childhood of Jesus. Luke wrote, *"And Jesus increased in wisdom and in stature, and in favor with God and man"* (Luke 2:52). In the Book of Hebrews, we read, *"Although He was a Son, He learned obedience through what He suffered"* (Hebrews 5:8). All of these verses leave us with the awareness that as Jesus set aside His omnipresence, so also He set aside His omniscience. Jesus *"emptied Himself,"* choosing to limit Himself to a human's knowledge and learning processes. He had no knowledge that is not available to you!

It is more challenging to comprehend Jesus as a human when we view His quality of omnipotence. As a human being, did Jesus have power because He is God? His miracles seem to indicate He had great Divine power! Did Jesus empty Himself of all the other attributes but decide to hold tightly to His power as God? If we believe Jesus *"emptied Himself"* of omnipotence, we must explain how He could do miracles and live in the spirit of Christmas. The answer becomes clear when we recognize that Jesus performed no miracles until John the Baptist baptized Him. Matthew records, *"And when Jesus was baptized, immediately He went up from the water, and behold, the heavens were opened to Him, and He saw the Spirit of God descending like a dove and coming to rest on Him"* (Matthew 3:16). Here is the secret! The Holy Spirit filled Jesus! What Jesus did, He did not do. It was the Father, through the Spirit, doing it through Him. Jesus did not do what He did because He was God; Jesus did what He did because He was a man filled with God! The second member of the Trinity God became a man and set aside, *"emptied Himself,"* of all He knew as God, to be a total human.

Jesus became the prototype of humanity. The spirit of Christmas in the heart of God wanted to give Himself to every individual. Jesus became the second Adam to blaze a trail back to what God intended in creating humanity in the beginning (Romans 5:12-19). As Man, Jesus had no advantage, extra power, or additional resources that are not available to us. The Spirit of God, the Spirit of Christmas, living in Jesus as Man can live in us! The nature of "get, grab, and protect" and "always think about yourself" is crucified with Christ. His Spirit, "bleed, suffer, and die," and "never think about yourself" can source our lives. We can know the life of Christmas!

Think of the sacrifice Jesus made for us in the spirit of Christmas. It is impossible to comprehend! Stretch your imagination with me. To understand the sacrifice, imagine a warehouse filled with millions of spiders. There are spiders of all sizes, shapes, and species. Imagine you have a special love for these spiders, the spirit of Christmas. Every day, you fellowship with and care for them. One day, you notice something is wrong. Sin has entered your spider world, evident by their actions. Groups of spiders have formed gangs. They are destroying other spiders. They have changed inside to "get, grab, and protect" and "always think about yourself." Someone must do something to stop this!

You try to communicate with the spiders. You speak to them directly, but they do not understand English. They simply regard your words as thunder. You write them a love letter, but they do not read English and do not bother opening the pages of your book. You create a lovely environment for them, but they destroy it without concern. Finally, it becomes evident that there is only one way to save them. You have to become a spider. You set aside all you know and enjoy as a human. You do not become Spiderman but think, speak, walk, eat, and live like a spider. You are a real spider.

You show the spiders the spirit of Christmas. By your lifestyle, you reveal to them the way spiders are to live. They see how different you are and despise you. They plot to kill you, finally nailing you to an eight-legged cross. But God raises you from the dead, and you return to the spider world. This illustration is silly and does not parallel the depth of what occurred in the incarnation. But think of what it would mean for you to become a spider and of all you would have to set aside. Even though becoming a spider would be a tremendous sacrifice, may I suggest that sacrifice is only a tiny percentage of Jesus's sacrifice to leave all He knew as God and become human?

But there is another primary consideration in the story. If you become a spider for three months and live to be ninety years old, your life as a spider would only be a minute portion of your overall life. Suppose you regain your humanity and all you enjoy as a human after three months as a spider. While giving up three months would be a great sacrifice, it does not compare to an eternal sacrifice of never returning to your human form. Eternal means forever, and your sacrifice for spiders means you will forever be a spider!

Is this the real story of the incarnation? Did Jesus, God, empty Himself to become an actual human? While He did not give up being God, did He give up every advantage He had as God? Can One give up what they have without giving up Who they are? Did Jesus embrace this sacrifice for a mere thirty-three years? Did He become one of us forever? Did Jesus become the first one of a whole new species of humanity called Sons of God who would live in the spirit of Christmas? Did not God raise Jesus from the dead as one of us? Did He not ascend to the Father's right hand as one of us? Is Jesus not reigning as King of the Kingdom as one of us? Will He not return the second time as one of us? He *"emptied Himself"* forever to become one with us!

Now, we must question the issue of motive. In our world of "get, grab, and protect" and "always think about yourself," there is always an angle. What is God's angle in making this sacrifice? What is the advantage? Is it money? Is my tithe what He wants? That is a preposterous thought! The Trinity God can turn streets into gold with the mere thought of Their creative mind. God does not need my money. Perhaps He is after my service. Think of the millions of man-hours given to God. That, too, is a ridiculous consideration. God created angels with nothing but service in mind. They can serve Him better, faster, and more efficiently than us.

What is God's motive? It is the spirit of Christmas (Philippians 2:1-4). It is the spirit of *"encouragement"* flowing consistently through Him that desires to strengthen and establish you. That comes from the resource of the *"comfort of love,"* which dominates His motive and will. He has no thought except what will benefit you! This is deep in His *"affection,"* residing in the core of His being. *"Mercy"* constantly moves Him to see you with a "bleed, suffer, and die" and "never think about yourself" spirit! It drove Jesus to empty Himself! Whatever the cost, however long the consequence, and whenever you experience pain, He loves you! That is the style of the cross! God's love demands He be redemptive.

This kind of *"emptied Himself"* demands a response. You cannot brush this aside as if it does not apply to you. God is confronting us with the spirit of Christmas found in Christ. This kind of love demands my total life. How can I possibly continue to live for myself? How can I think of continuing in "get, grab, and protect" and "always think about myself?" He must fill me with His heart. His Spirit must cleanse and redeem me from myself! Anyone who loves me with this kind of selfless love can be trusted! I must surrender to Him! Anything less would be a mockery in the face of Jesus' sacrifice for me! Lukewarmness makes all He did cheap and insignificant. You understand what the author of Hebrews meant when he wrote, *"They are crucifying once again the Son of God to their own harm and holding Him up to contempt"* (Hebrews 6:6). We cannot compromise. We cannot give only a part of our lives.

We dare not give our lives to Jesus to "get, grab, and protect" and "always think about myself." I must not grasp His redemptive love for selfish reasons. I must acknowledge my self-centeredness and abandon myself without condition. I must come to Him with "bleed, suffer, and die" and "never think about myself." It is the Spirit of Christmas!

4

THE POINT OF DEATH

Philippians 2:8

"And being found in human form, he humbled himself by becoming obedient to the point of death, even death on a cross" *(Philippians 2:8).*

Two spirits, mindsets, or perspectives operate throughout human life. These two views are in extreme opposition and cannot dwell together. One drive declares a major war to destroy the other. The spirit of Christmas is the heart of God expressed in Jesus. His birth to His death gives adequate details to the spirit of "bleed, suffer, and die" and "never think about yourself." You cannot live for yourself and have the mind of Christ! In this mindset, there are no thoughts to eliminate, ruin, or destroy but to redeem, change, and rescue. The opposite spirit is the demonic nature of "grab, get, demand, and protect" and "always think about yourself." This attitude must seek to destroy everything that contradicts it. Therefore, the demonic spirit declares war upon the spirit of Christmas!

This conflict occurs in the spiritual realm, the natural universes around us, our nation, and our personal lives. The battle rages greater than we know. Paul illustrates it in Jesus! He begins with Jesus is God (Philippians 2:6). He is the objective reality of God. He is God-filled with the spirit of Christmas. This spirit is generated from His nature, producing another objective reality. God became Man (Philippians 2:7). The spirit of Christmas in the heart of God demanded the setting aside of all He had to be redemptive to humanity. How will this same spirit of Christmas display itself in His humanity? That is the content of our passage.

He begins with *"And,"* the first Greek word in the Greek text, a translation of the Greek word "kai." *"And"* links our verse with the preceding verse, indicating more information on the same subject. Immediately, Paul declares, *"being found in human form,"* reaffirming everything he just said about God becoming human. The Greek word "heurisko" is translated as *"being found."* In the New Testament, the idea of finding links with the verb "seeking." They become complementary verbs, meaning two verbs with different meanings brought together to form one idea. In relationship to God, we have discovered that the determining factor in "seeking and finding" is God Himself. It is not a matter of my ability or careful searching techniques; God determines my finding. Seeking is an internal response to my heart's desiring. God recognizes this desire and allows me to find it. "Finding" is not a self-effort, a matter of fate or luck, but a result of the spirit of Christmas in the heart of God. The "bleed, suffer, and die" and "never think about yourself" spirit drives the activities of God, causing Him to reveal Himself to me when I respond with an open heart. If I seek with my whole heart, I will find Him. It is impossible to seek Him and not find Him! He seeks me and waits for the response of my heart.

Paul declares that we found Jesus in human form. He was not hiding, and we did not have to search; He did not establish obstacles to hinder us, but we made our way through the maze to discover Him. Jesus planted Himself in the middle of our humanity! He assumed conception, and Mary brought Him into our physical world through the pain of childbirth. Jesus assumed the helplessness and dependency of a baby upon His mother. He came into our histories. He had a birth certificate recorded at the courthouse. He was counted in the census as we are. He had a grandpa, as we do. He is one of us! He planted Himself amid our time, for all time revolves around Him, before and after His birth (BC and AD)! The objective reality of our human Jesus was not the result of our scholarship, careful investigation, or inventive spirit. The spirit of Christmas revealed Jesus to us in the flesh!

The word *"form"* appears again in our passage, a translation from the Greek word "schema." The English word *"form"* is used three times (Philippians 2:6, 7, 8). However, in verse eight, Paul uses a different word than the first two times. There is an argument among scholars about the emphasis of these different Greek words (morphe and schema). Some say that the first two references (morphe) focus on the internal essence while this third (schema) focuses on the external appearance. Others boldly state that we must not make such a distinction. We do know this: the word *"form"* (schema) is directly related to humanity because Paul uses the Greek word "anthropos," which means "man." Paul states that the humanity of Jesus is an objective reality!

The living proof of the objective reality is *"He humbled Himself."* The verb *"humbled"* translates from the Greek word "tapeinoo," meaning to bring low, to humble, or abase. *"Himself"* is a direct object receiving the action of the humbling, a reflexive pronoun denoting mutual participation in an act on the part of the verb's subject. The verb is in the active voice, meaning the subject is responsible for the verb's action. Therefore, there is a strong emphasis by Paul to reveal that the spirit of Christmas in Jesus produced the action of not only joining humanity but of humbling Himself within the human realm. *"He humbled Himself"* by becoming a human slave, and now, as a slave, He humbles Himself even further.

Do not miss the wonder of the humiliation! As God, Jesus humbled Himself to be birthed (ginomai) in the objective reality as human, now as a human, *"He humbled Himself."* The spirit of Christmas, the nature of God, is once again demonstrating itself! This humiliation is *"by becoming obedient to the point of death."* The Greek word "ginomai" is translated as *"being born"* in verse seven and is translated as *"by becoming"* in verse eight. The generating life behind all of this is the spirit of Christmas, the heart of God's nature. Paul adds in this phrase, *"to the point of death."* The Greek word "mechri" is translated as *"to the point."* It is used metaphorically for degree or extent. The spirit of Christmas drove Jesus to the extreme of whatever was necessary to complete the redemptive mission.

THE POINT OF DEATH

The climax of the statement is in the use of the word *"death."* Paul states, *"to the point of death"* and *"death of the cross,"* making it the statement's climax. Paul highlights a distinct progression flowing from the spirit of Christmas. God became Man, but not just a man. He became a slave, not just a slave, but a slave embracing death. But He did not simply embrace death, but the death of a cross! Paul took us from the objective reality of Jesus as God to the objective reality of a Man embracing the worst of death. In both cases, *"death"* is translated from the Greek word "thanatos." Paul does not describe Jesus quietly bowing His head and ceasing to breathe. Throughout the Scriptures, "thanatos" has the sense of destruction, hell, misery, and exclusion from the presence and merger with God.

The early Church fathers called this "the Divine Scandal"! God, the highest of glory and holiness, was so controlled by love that He redeemed and rescued us and has taken on our flesh. He did not become a King but a slave. He became the most vile of slaves, embracing the curse of the law by dying on a cross. Do you understand that no one to whom Paul writes had a gold cross around their neck? No one in Philippi used the cross as a symbol of their faith! They did not erect the cross in their sanctuaries; that was scandalous and embarrassing! The Best became the Worst!

To grasp this action, we must understand the concept of "assumption." No one can redeem what they do not assume. "Assuming" means "to acquire, take on, adopt, come to have." Jesus, who is God, humbled Himself and assumed humanity as a slave. In the context of One who is owned and mastered by the Divine nature of love in the heart of God, He assumed the position of sin.

THE POSITION OF SIN

But Jesus never sinned Himself, which makes this all the more incredible! *"For we do not have a high priest who is unable to sympathize with our weaknesses, but One who in every respect has been tempted as we are, yet without sin"* (Hebrews 4:15). *"For our sake He made Him to be sin Who knew no sin, so that in Him we might become the righteousness of God"* (2 Corinthians 5:21). Who can understand this? We describe this reality in the curse of death found on a cross.

We must understand this assumption in the context of what Paul describes in this passage (Philippians 2:1-11). By his language, Paul forces us to embrace Jesus as God, *"He was in the form of God"* (Philippians 2:6). He was not a part of God, a partial God, or a fake God. Jesus was the objective reality of God! Everything God is Jesus possesses, for He is God! *"But emptied Himself, by taking the form of a servant, being born in the likeness of men"* (Philippians 2:7). The same concept of "objective reality" applies to Jesus being God, and we must apply it to Jesus being human. He was not a fake god; He was not a fake man! Now Jesus has gone to the extreme, to *"the point of death, even death on a cross"* (Philippians 2:8). Must this not be considered "objective reality" as well? As a child, I was exposed to pictures of Jesus on the cross with a massive burden of sin on His shoulders. Was sin a mere wart on His toe, a burden on His back to bear for a time? Was He a fake god, a fake man, or a fake sinner?

Let's go back to Paul's statement: *"For our sake He made Him to be sin Who knew no sin"* (2 Corinthians 5:21). The Greek word translated as *"made"* is "poieo!" "Poieo" is the Greek word for "doing," which involves the nature. In our Philippians passage, Paul does not describe sin in terms of activities or deeds but nature. The nature of God in Christ is a driving love that reaches into our lives to build, enhance, and fulfill. It is a "bleed, suffer, and die" and "never think about yourself" nature. Paul contrasts that nature with *"selfish ambition and conceit,"* a "grab, get, demand, protect" and "always think about yourself" nature (Philippians 2:3). The evil nature demonstrates itself in the actions of the worst kind from sexual perversion, murder, and all works of the flesh (Galatians 5:19-21). But equally as bad are the charitable deeds done with self-centered motives, prayers filled with selfish desire, and fasting determined to convince God to grant our selfish needs (Matthew 6). Did Jesus assume the guilt of the *"nature of children of wrath"* (Ephesians 2:3)? Did He become self-centered, had to have His way, always thinking about Himself as I am? Did He assume all the guilt of my evil, selfish nature in objective reality? Did the driving force of God's love nature drive Him to the extreme, radical, complete embrace of who I am? Does this bring us to some understanding of Jesus' final cries from the cross, *"My God, my God, why have you forsaken me"* (Matthew 27:46)?

THE PENALTY OF SIN

If Jesus assumed "the position of sin," then you must agree Jesus assumed the penalty of sin. One who has never sinned and will never experience the damnation of sin assumed the full consequence of all sin. It is incomprehensible to imagine a human being who was never touched by the defeating, destructive, damning consequence of sin suddenly embracing the full results of the world's raw sewage of sin from all generations. We face the meaning of *"death,"* as found in our passage (Philippians 2:8). This is the Divine scandal! He did not merely *"become obedient to the point of death,"* but the content of that death was *"death on a cross"* (Philippians 2:8).

In the historical view of Jesus' time, Romans used the cross to satisfy their primitive lust for revenge and sadistic cruelty. As we know from the Scriptural account of Jesus, they associated crucifixion with other forms of torture, including flogging. They would torture the criminal for days in unspeakable ways until death. By the first-century standards, no experience was more loathsomely degrading than this. According to Jewish law, anyone crucified died under the curse of God (Deuteronomy 21:23; Galatians 3:13). History reports that in polite Roman society, the word "cross" was an obscenity, not to be uttered in conversation.

The cross is a physical expression of sin's destruction in human life. In today's self-centered destruction exhibited in the terror attacks on Jews, we have become aware of it again. Murder, raping of women, and beheading of babies makes us shrink in horror. How could "grab, get, demand, and protect" and "always think about yourself" wholly dominate a human being? What will this self-centered nature do in the eternal spiritual world we will all experience? What will be the full consequence of this nature when it is turned loose without the presence of God? The Scriptures labels it "hell!"

We cannot explain the depth of the sinful nature. Imagine God, whose nature is helping, building, enhancing, and strengthening, assuming the objective reality of humanity with a sinful nature. He dwells in a world of people who, in the self-centered sin, "grab, get, demand, and protect" and "always think about themselves." To transform them from their evil nature to His nature, Jesus had to assume not only the guilt of their sin but sin's total penalty and consequence. I can pay the full penalty for my self-centered nature. I can spend eternity in the destruction, damnation, and ruin of my cancerous selfishness. You can do the same. But who could pay the penalty for both you and me? No one dominated by his sinful, selfish nature can make such a payment. Jesus, who is God, became the Man without the evil nature. But who can assume the consequences of every man's sin? Only God, the Infinite One, can embrace the finite race of humanity. Jesus is God and Man embracing our penalty!

THE POWER OF SIN

My head is spinning over the wonder of what Paul declared, yet he has more to declare. Jesus assumed "the position of sin," "the penalty of sin," and the power of sin. Throughout the New Testament, the writer's personify *"death"* as a person who reigns over us. The writer of the Book of Hebrews reveals a picture of the struggle involved within us who are in bondage to the power of death and sin. *"Since therefore the children share in flesh and blood, He Himself likewise partook of the same things, that through death He might destroy the one who has the power of death, that is, the devil, and deliver all those who through fear of death were subject to lifelong slavery"* (Hebrews 2:14-15). Jesus, a Man who never sinned Himself, takes within Himself the dominating power of the selfish nature of sin. The power of this destructive, damning nature gleefully tries to trap Him. In his Pentecost sermon, Peter illustrated it as gigantic fingers of destruction and hell reaching out to hold Jesus in bondage (Acts 2:24). They want to imprison Him in the eternal damnation of death. But the roaring life of the Holy Spirit dwelling and merging with this Man releases Him. *"Death"* cannot hold Him. He is raised from death, conquering the power of death!

The first man, Adam, was faced with this same battle. The temptation of the self-centered nature of being your own god embraced him and conquered the father of all humankind. We have all been thrust into this same domination and are destined for the lifelong destruction of the power of sin. It ruins our families, destroys our relationships, shrivels our spirits, depresses our emotions, twists our thinking, and eternally destroys our souls. But another Man came (Romans 5)! He is in Adam's original position before the fall; He is without the domination and power of sin. Jesus willingly engages in the fierce battle with the power of sin. The devil used every weapon he had against Jesus, the Man, but could not defeat Him. Satan presented Jesus with physical pleasure, prosperity, fame in ministry, and even complete rulership of all the world's kingdoms (Matthew 4:1-11). But Jesus, filled with the Spirit of God, marched on fulfilling the destiny of the nature of God. Finally, the devil got out his greatest weapon, *"death."* Jesus readily embraces *"the point of death, even death on a cross."* The power of death drug Jesus into the very depths of the underworld (1 Peter 3:19). But all the self-centered power of death could not hold Him. Jesus marched into the eternities, conquering hell and death.

What does this mean to us? We are *"in Jesus"* (Philippians 2:1, 5). His conquering nature has become ours! As He conquered through the fullness of the Spirit, we likewise *"are more than conquerors through Him who loved us"* and gave Himself for us (Romans 8:37). His mind is our mind; we think like Him (Philippians 2:5).

5

HIGHLY EXALTED

Philippians 2:9

"Therefore God has highly exalted Him and bestowed on Him the name that is above every name" *(Philippians 2:9).*

Although Paul has given us many interesting insights, we must constantly remember the main thrust of the passage is the "spirit of Christmas" in the heart of God. In the first two verses, he presents the mindset. The nature of God consistently acts to strengthen and establish us in the dream and purpose for which God created us. The nature of God's deep internal love produces the action. This "gut level" love of God's inner being is a hand-wringing, anxious compassion that drives His intent. Paul links the "spirit of Christmas" with the "spirit of crucifixion," not a seasonal thing, but the consistent expression of who God is! It is a "bleed, suffer, and die" and "never think about yourself" attitude.

Paul contrasts this mindset with **"selfish ambition and conceit"** (Philippians 2:3), a demonic spirit that "gets, grabs, demands, and protects" and "always thinks about itself." No one can be a Kingdom person and have this attitude. It is so contrary to the nature of God there is no tolerance for its presence. Like oil and water, they will not mix. Even if the demonic nature tries to adapt to the activities of God's nature, the motivation never changes. Therefore, without His nature at the core of my being, even my most religious deeds become sin!

Paul illustrates the nature of God in Christ. He begins by establishing the unchangeable fact that Jesus is God (Philippians 2:6). Jesus *"was in the form of God,"* meaning He is the objective reality of God. Because Jesus has the nature of God, He *"emptied Himself"* (Philippians 2:7). Everything He possessed that did not correspond with being human, Jesus set aside. But His humiliation was not merely that he became human; in His humanity, Jesus became a slave (Philippians 2:7). But He was not simply a slave, but was further humiliated by embracing the extremity of death, *"even the death of a cross"* (Philippians 2:8). It is the Divine scandal!

Suddenly, the subject of the action changes from Jesus to God! Do not get confused; Jesus never ceased being God! Therefore, from the beginning of the plan, the subject becomes the Trinity God. These two statements, *"has highly exalted Him,"* and *"bestowed on Him the name that is above every name"* (Philippians 2:9), reveal the Trinity God's actions. These are not two separate activities; the first describes the second, and the second describes the first.

Paul begins with *"Therefore,"* a translation of two Greek words, "dio" and "kai." The first two Greek words in the text are not the usual words translated as "therefore." "Dio" is a superordinating (hyperordinating) inferential conjunction. An inferential conjunction states the conclusion of a previously mentioned matter. The glossary of "Fribergs' Analytical Greek New Testament reads, "A superordinating conjunction is a word that casts the clause it heads into a superordinate relationship to some other (subordinated) clause." A superordinate clause is "a grammatical construction related to but more prominent than another clause related to it." That means that the exaltation of Jesus becomes superior to the humiliation of Jesus. It is not superior in importance, for both are equally significant. The exaltation is not superior in necessity, for both must occur to redeem humanity. The exaltation is superior only because the crucifixion is defeated without the resurrection, ascension, and sitting at the right hand of God! While the miles traveled on the journey are essential, they mean nothing if you do not arrive.

The Trinity God *"has highly exalted Him,"* a translation of the Greek word "hyperypsose." It is a compound word that includes "huper," meaning above or high, and "hupsoo," which expresses elevation. The Greek word "huper" links forty times with words in the New Testament, and twenty-eight of them are in Paul's writings. In most cases, they magnify or express excess, not position. Paul relates Jesus' exaltation with clear and vividly explicit details. He states that Jesus' exaltation is a super exaltation! Nowhere else in the New Testament does "hyperypsose" appear!

The primary verb "hupsoo" is often used in the New Testament to describe the exaltation of Jesus. During Jesus' conversation with Nicodemus, Jesus used the term for the action of Moses lifting the bronze serpent on a pole for all to see (John 3:14; Numbers 21:9). Peter uses this verb to describe Jesus elevated to the right hand of God and receiving the promise from the Father to pour out His Spirit upon us (Acts 2:33). In addressing the Sanhedrin, Peter defends their continual preaching and teaching in the name of Jesus by declaring the exaltation of Jesus to the right hand of God to be Leader and Savior (Acts 5:31).

Paul immediately launches into another clear and explicit statement concerning this exaltation, *"and bestowed on Him the name that is above every name"* (Philippians 2:9). The Greek word "charizomai" is translated as *"bestowed."* It comes from the Greek word "charis," which means "grace!" The grace that so graciously extends to us salvation, *"by grace you have been saved,"* is also involved in the exaltation of Jesus. It is the nature of God to "bleed, suffer, and die" and "never think about yourself." The spirit of Christmas manifested in Jesus' birth is demonstrated in His death and flows through the Trinity God in "bestowing" upon Jesus a superior name!

Paul uses the language in this verse to clearly define the details of Jesus' exaltation.

THE EXALTED MANHOOD

Paul thoroughly established the objective reality of Jesus being God. Jesus *"was in the form of God"* (Philippians 2:6). The Greek word "morphe" is translated as *"form."* Paul uses this same word in connection with the humanity of Jesus, *"taking the form of a servant, being born in the likeness of men"* (Philippians 2:7). Jesus is not a "shapeshifter" who can change His appearance at will. The Greek word "morphe" refers to the essence of the representation. It suggests an expression of something that reflects or manifests fully, honestly, and permanently the essence of what something is! Jesus is the objective reality of God manifested in humanity; *"He is the image of the invisible God"* (Colossians 1:15). No one can be in the form of God who is not God. However, "morphe" is not merely shaping an idea, concept, or attitude. It is the utterance of the inner life or personality, a life that bespeaks the existence of God. Jesus has been in this *"form"* from eternity (John 17:5).

Since Jesus is truly God, how can someone exalt Him? No position or throne is higher or more significant than He already occupies! How can God exalt God? The writer of the Book of Hebrews quotes the Old Testament concerning Jesus,

> *"Your throne, O God, is forever and ever, the scepter of uprightness is the scepter of Your kingdom"* (Hebrews 1:8).

However, The Trinity God did not exalt Jesus as God but as Man! This reality bespeaks the amazing fact of the eternal state of Jesus' humiliation. God *"emptied Himself"* of everything that distinguished Him from us. He did not give up who He is but gave up what He had. He set aside every advantage He had as God beyond us. In that humiliation, He took *"the form of a servant."* He did not cling to the highest position as a human but became a "Slave." As a "Slave," Jesus pushed the limits of sacrifice *"to the point of death."* But it was not merely a ceasing to breathe, but a Divine scandal, *"even the death on a cross!"*

Jesus assumed our sin. After all the humiliation, destruction, ruin, and complete annihilation of that assumption, the Trinity God raised Jesus from the dead, the destruction! His resurrection was not the resurrection of God, although Jesus is always God. It is the resurrection of Man filled with God! Jesus, the Man, was raised from the dead! This same Man ascended, *"and a cloud took Him out of their sight"* (Acts 1:9). There were two individuals in white robes standing by the disciples who asked, *"Men of Galilee, why do you stand looking into heaven? This Jesus, who was taken up from you into heaven, will come in the same way as you saw Him go into heaven"* (Acts 1:11). He will return in the second coming as a Man!

Peter told the Sanhedrin in the second phase of persecution, *"God exalted Him at His right hand as Leader and Savior"* (Acts 5:31). Jesus did not return to heaven to receive back all He *"emptied Himself"* of but was exalted by God in His humiliation as Man. Jesus is the prototype of all we are to be in Him. The Trinity God points to Jesus, saying, "This is what I intend you to be!" Jesus is a Man filled with God's Spirit, displaying God's heart. Was this not what God created the first Adam to be? Was this not what sinned destroyed through the self-centered demonic nature? Is this not what Jesus conquered in His death and redeemed us to become?

The Trinity God exalts Jesus as the second Adam, the first Man to make it. He has re-established our destiny. Jesus restored us to our rightful place in God's design. We are His brothers (Hebrews 2:11). He is our King, but He is our Man King! One of us has made it to the right hand of God and has given us direct access to the heart of God! We are no longer orphans in rebellion and alone. *"He chose us in Him before the foundation of the world, that we should be holy and blameless before Him. In love He predestined us for adoption to Himself as sons through Jesus Christ, according to the purpose of His will, to the praise of His glorious grace, with which He has blessed us in the Beloved"* (Ephesians 1:4-6).

THE EXALTED MESSAGE

While the issue of exaltation focuses on the Person of Jesus in His humanity, the undercurrent of the exaltation is the heart of God expressed through this Person. That is the structure of Paul's presentation. He contrasts the "spirit of Christmas" and the "demonic spirit." He contrasts the "bleed, suffer, die" and "never think about yourself" heart of God with the "grab, get, demand, and protect" and "always think about yourself" demonic spirit. A Man filled with the Spirit of God, demonstrating the heart of God, and merged with the expressions of God is exalted!

The "spirit of Christmas" wins!!! The Spirit of God filled Jesus (Matthew 3:13-17). Then the temptation began (Matthew 4:1-11). It was a spiritual battle raging through the physical life of Jesus. After forty days of extreme spiritual warfare, Jesus became intensely aware of His physical hunger. Immediately, the devil seized the opportunity. Had Jesus not *"emptied Himself"* of all his resources as God and become dependent upon the Spirit of God dwelling in Him? Was He not reliant on God for every aspect of His life, even the physical realm? It indeed is not working out very well if He is starving. "Bleed, suffer, and die" and "never think about yourself" are not meeting His needs. The devil suggests that Jesus no longer depends on God for His needs but "grab, get, demand, and protect" and "always think about Himself." He could grab His Divine powers, which are still His because He is God. For this moment of great need, He could use them for Himself. What a great temptation!

Jesus is at the pinnacle of the temple. All of His ministry to win the world stretches out before Him. Where does He begin? The devil seizes the moment and suggests He do the spectacular action, "grab, get, demand, and protect," and "always think about yourself." He could leap off the pinnacle, and angels would rescue Him, impressing the crowds. He could jump from the pinnacle of the temple where the priest blew the horn announcing the sacrifice offering. If He remained at the pinnacle, He would "bleed, suffer, and die" and "never think about Himself." Don't remain there; think about yourself! What a great temptation!

The devil took Jesus to the highest of world positions and offered Him all the Kingdoms of the world. All He had to do was to embrace the demonic spirit, "grab, get, demand, and protect," and "always think about yourself." After all, the kingdoms of the world were dominated by and expressed this spirit. Murders, rape, hatred, envy, and every other action defined by the demonic mindset were present. Jesus could embrace this attitude and rule over the Kingdoms of destruction and hell. Will He abandon His call to return the world to "bleed, suffer, and die" and "never think about yourself?"

He has fiercely embraced the heart of God! Now, God exalted Jesus to His right hand! But it is not simply a physical exaltation; the heart of God has conquered!

Humanity is restored from destruction to construction. The heart of God, which builds, establishes, and enhances, is released into the lives of humanity. As the dust settles, Jesus reigns as King! "Bleed, suffer, and die" and "never think about yourself" wins!!! It is important to note that in our passage, there is no indication that Jesus merely endured the humiliation for the sake of the exaltation. He did not become Man so God could crown Him King. If that were true, the humbling would not have been true humiliation; it would have been self-regarding, not self-denying. Paul says, ***"God has highly exalted Him and bestowed on Him the name that is above every name"*** (Philippians 2:9). It was "given" to Him. He did not earn it; it is grace!

"Bleed, suffer, and die" and "never think about yourself" do not serve for rewards. The very thought of "what do I get" destroys the core of the heart of God. Are there rewards for the Christian? Absolutely! But the one who gets them is the one who does not want them. Is it not enough to know His heart, merge with His nature, and share His mind? Is His life not sufficient?

THE EXALTED MINISTRY

Our verse focuses on the "function of the Person," not merely the "state of the Person." In other words, the focus is not simply on Jesus, the Human God is exalting. The focus is on the heart of God demonstrated through the Person of Jesus. But "bleed, suffer, and die" and "never think about yourself" are not simply states of existence but always spill forth in ministry. By its very nature, it demands action! This action always has the characteristic of the heart of God. As the Trinity God, driven by His nature to act on our behalf, the exalted Jesus cannot idly lounge on a throne in comfort.

Jesus' exaltation was not "retirement!" In finishing His task of redemption on a physical earth, He did not ascend to the heavenly realms to "play eternal shovelboard." *"Therefore He had to be made like His brothers in every respect, so that He might become a merciful and faithful High Priest in the service of God, to make propitiation for the sins of the people. For because He Himself has suffered when tempted, He is able to help those who are being tempted"* (Hebrews 2:17-18). Peter, explaining Pentecost to the questioning crowd, cried, *"Being therefore exalted at the right hand of God, and having received from the Father the promise of the Holy Spirit, He has poured out this that you yourselves are seeing and hearing"* (Acts 2:33). Who administrates the fullness of God through the Spirit to the believer? It is the Exalted One! The merger of my heart and life with the "bleed, suffer, and die" and "never think about yourself" Spirit of God is under the control and direction of Jesus!

The redemptive ministry of God's heart, displayed in the humiliation of Jesus, now reigns as King of the Kingdom, demonstrating itself through my life, His Body! We are the humiliation of Christ functioning in our neighborhood. We do not minister for Him in talented displays of self-centeredness. We are an extension of "bleed, suffer, die" and "never think about yourself." It is the spirit of Christmas!

6

GRACE

Philippians 2:9

"Therefore God has highly exalted Him and bestowed on Him the name that is above every name" *(Philippians 2:9).*

In all of Paul's writings, the immensity of God's love captures him. The size of God's love is not his focus, for he cannot measure it. The amount of God's love is not the issue, for he cannot weigh it. The total has not captured him, for he cannot mathematically add it. He writes, **"Who shall separate us from the love of Christ? Shall tribulation, or distress, or persecution, or famine, or nakedness, or danger, or sword"** (Romans 8:35)? The captivating strength of God's love is within the nature of His inner heart. This description of Paul illuminates the inner core of God's being.

This inner state of being is **"in Christ"** (Philippians 2:1). Every expression of Jesus is one of **"encouragement,"** the flow of love that wants to establish, enhance, and support. This flow comes from the inner heart of the *"comfort of love."* Jesus participates in the fullness of the Spirit, the nature of God. This *"affection"* is in the "gut level" of God's existence. The New Testament consistently uses various words and illustrations to portray the nature of God. How can we describe the indescribable? Each time we speak of it, the desperate awareness of inadequacy is present!

One inadequate expression of God's nature is "grace." "Grace" is a feminine noun "charis," coming from "chairo," meaning "to rejoice." The nature of God freely expresses His loving-kindness to men, and His only motive is in the bounty and benevolence of His heart. "Grace" is an unearned and unmerited favor. Grace stands in direct antithesis to works; the two are mutually exclusive. Paul captures this antithesis in his contrast of the "spirit of Christmas" and the "demonic spirit." *"Selfish ambition or conceit"* is the spirit of "earn, merit, and deserve," an attitude that nullifies any experience of grace! The mind of Christ is "bleed, suffer, and die" and "never think about yourself;" the demonic spirit is "get, grab, demand, and protect" and "always think about yourself."

Paul magnificently illustrates this "grace" in Christ. How do we fully comprehend the driving force of God's loving heart? Jesus assumed the flesh of humanity. He is not a fake God, and neither is He a fake man! Assuming humanity, Jesus took the objective reality of "slave" to the extreme, *"even death on a cross"* (Philippians 2:8). Paul gives two statements that explain each other. *"God has highly exalted Him"* and *"bestowed on Him the name that is above every name"* (Philippians 2:9). Jesus is God; therefore, His exaltation cannot be in that capacity. God exalted Jesus in His humanity. The discovery of His humanity continuing into the eternal realm is incomprehensible, declaring the depth of the mindset in God's nature. How ridiculous to embrace Jesus in His assumption of slavery and death for humanity and project He will return in anger, wrath, and revenge. Has His nature changed? Did the loving Jesus who wanted to enhance, establish, and support change His mind and thus His nature?

While there is much to discuss in that reality, our investigation focuses on the second statement, *"bestowed on Him the name that is above every name"* (Philippians 2:9). This insight clarifies the exaltation of Jesus. The Greek word "charizomai" is translated as *"bestowed."* It comes from the Greek word "charis," which means "grace!" The grace that so graciously extends to us salvation, *"by grace you have been saved,"* is also involved in the exaltation of Jesus. It is the nature of God that is "bleed, suffer, and die" and "never think about yourself." The spirit of Christmas manifested in Jesus' birth is demonstrated in His death and flows through the Trinity God in "bestowing" upon Jesus a superior name!

"Charizomai" is used twenty-three times in the New Testament; the writings of Paul claim eleven of those appearances. According to the many translations available, "charizomai" is only translated one of two ways, "given" or *"bestowed."* The idea of "giving something" opens the opportunity for an abundance of motives. However, *"bestowed"* narrows those possibilities. "Grace" properly understood can only be expressed by the nature of "bleed, suffer, and die" and "never think about yourself!" Jesus, as an exalted Man, experienced the "grace" of the Trinity God, establishing a parallel.

A PARALLEL

For the sake of clarity, we must understand that Jesus is God! He is not a little God, part of God, one-third God, but He is totally God. Whatever God is, Jesus is! *"He was in the form of God"* (Philippians 2:6). Jesus *"emptied Himself"* of everything that did not fit into being a man, *"taking the form of a servant, being born in the likeness of men"* (Philippians 2:7). This establishes a parallel between Jesus and me! I get hungry; Jesus got hungry. I need sleep; Jesus needed sleep. I have difficulty in relationships with others; Jesus dealt with conflicts within His relationships. I dwell in poverty in the spiritual realm, without resources (Matthew 5:3). I am helpless; Jesus is helpless. Was He not dependent upon His Father for every aspect of His life? Am I not reliant on Jesus for every part of my life? The relationship between God and man is never equal. I do not produce half of the relationship and God the other half. It is never I do my part and then God does His part! There is no earn, merit, or deserve within the relationship. I am helpless and dependent, and Jesus joined me in this condition as a Man!

Jesus expressed this need repeatedly. In describing His helplessness, He said, *"Truly, truly, I say to you, the Son can do nothing of His own accord"* (John 5:19). He proposed that the need of you and me is the resources and fullness of the Spirit He experienced. Abiding must take place, *"for apart from Me you can do nothing"* (John 15:5). Note the prayer Jesus offered to the Father before His death, *"I in them and You in Me, that they may become perfectly one, so that the world may know*

that You sent Me and loved them even as You loved Me"
(John 17:23). The same way the Father was in Jesus is the
same way Jesus is in me!

The same love the Father has for Jesus is the same
love I receive in quality and quantity. In this same prayer,
Jesus restated this reality as if it was essentially important,
*"I made known to them Your name, and I will continue
to make it known, that the love with which You have
loved Me may be in them, and I in them"* (John 17:26).
Is He not receiving what I am receiving, because our
helplessness is the same? These are not ideas or isolated
statements: *"As the Father has loved Me, so have I loved
you"* (John 15:9). *"As the Father has sent Me, even so
I am sending you"* (John 20:21). Is there a parallel
between Jesus' needs and my needs, my helplessness
and His helplessness, and the design of His life and
my design?

According to the Scriptures, I can only explain my life's
supply in terms of "grace!" *"For by grace you have been
saved through faith. And this is not of your own doing; it
is a gift of God, not a result of works, so that no one may
boast"* (Ephesians 2:8-9). *"For all have sinned and fall
short of the glory of God, and are justified by His grace
as a gift, through the redemption that is in Christ Jesus"*
(Romans 3:23-24). *"Grace"* is the opposite of earning, as
so forcibly stated in these verses. I am helpless; therefore,
I must receive. In His humanity, is Jesus in this same
situation? Was His life the result of the *"grace"* of God?
Was He raised from the dead by the *"grace"* of God? Was
He exalted by the *"grace"* of God?

Our passage states that God *"bestowed on Him."*
As previously noted, the Greek word "charizomai" is

translated as *"bestowed."* "Charizomai" is the middle voice of "charis," translated as *"grace."* Jesus, who is God, became man! As Man, He experienced the constant need for the *"grace"* of the Trinity God. The *"grace"* of God enveloped His death and resurrection. Paul says that even His exaltation resulted from the Trinity's *"grace."* In the eternal realm, Jesus experiences the *"grace"* of God.

"He who did not spare His own Son but gave Him up for us all, how will He not also with Him graciously give us (charizomai) *all things"* (Romans 8:32)? In this verse, Paul says we are *"with Him."* Has He not merged with us both in the spiritual and physical realms? Because of this merger, we also receive everything the Trinity God is "graciously giving" or "bestowing" upon Jesus. One cannot fathom the immensity of such a thought! *"The Spirit Himself bears witness with our spirit that we are children of God, and if children then heirs - heirs of God and fellow heirs with Christ"* (Romans 8:16-17). We are the recipients of the gracious benevolence of the spirit of Christmas. The "bleed, suffer, and die" and "never think about yourself" *"grace"* of God working in Jesus is now working in and for us!

Victory permeates every fiber of the marvelous story of Jesus! Carefully consider the consistent threat present in every event of the life of Jesus' humanity. The destructive force of demonic efforts was constantly at work in His birth and childhood. Suddenly, Caesar Augustus declares a decree that all the world should be registered (Luke 2:1). Was it not a demonic plot to cast Mary into an arduous journey in the final days of her pregnancy? Was Jesus not condemned to be born in a dirty, germ-filled stable

(Luke 2:16)? Herod the King exerted all of his military force to destroy this Babe (Matthew 2:13). How is this Child still alive? The intervention of God's grace on His behalf is the answer!

The moment Jesus stepped into ministry, the entire demonic forces raged in battle against Him in the wilderness temptation (Matthew 4:1-11). Death threats were a constant part of the earthly ministry of Jesus (Matthew 12:14; Luke 4:29; John 11:53). The hatred and anger of the Jews built until they demanded Jesus' crucifixion. God finally allowed the demonic spirit of "grab, get, demand, and protect" and "always think about yourself" to overtake Jesus. Now the demonic force of hell and death have captured Him, BUT the grace of the Trinity God will bring victory to the life of Christ: God raised Jesus from the dead and exalted Him!

In Him, we have this same confidence! Is not the demonic nature doing everything possible to devour us? Are there not daily obstacles designed to bring us to defeat? BUT the same grace of the Trinity God working in and for Jesus is now ours! We are *"in Christ"* (Philippians 2:1). The nature of God, "bleed, suffer, and die," and "never think about yourself," is working in us, releasing the power of God in every obstacle. As Jesus lived in constant victory, so do we! Carefully note Paul's declaration:

> *"But we have this treasure in jars of clay, to show that the surpassing power belongs to God and not to us. We are afflicted in every way, but not crushed; perplexed, but not driven to despair; persecuted, but not forsaken; struck down, but*

not destroyed; always carrying in the body the death of Jesus, so that the life of Jesus may also be manifested in our bodies" *(2 Corinthians 4:7-10).*

There is nothing but victory for us! The Spirit of Christmas, the grace of God, is ours!

A PROBLEM

There is a massive problem. The grace of God simply does not make sense to the demonic spirit. The mindset of "grab, get, demand, and protect" and "always think about yourself" cannot grasp the Divine logic of "bleed, suffer, and die" and "never think about yourself." Jesus told the story of the master of a house who went out early in the morning to hire laborers for his vineyard (Matthew 20:1-15). The laborers agreed to work for a denarius a day. About the third hour (9 am), the owner saw other workers standing in the marketplace and hired them. He did the same at the sixth hour (noon) and the ninth hour (3 pm). Even at the eleventh hour of the day (5 pm), he found some idle and hired them. At the close of the work day, the owner paid each laborer the same, a denarius. Those who had worked all day were irate, even though they had agreed to the wage. It just isn't fair! Why? Can't the owner pay any compensation he desires? Did they not agree to the wage at the beginning of the day? But "grab, get, demand, and protect" and "always think about yourself" cannot accept the amazing grace of the owner.

Jesus told the story of the prodigal son who squandered his inheritance in riotous living and had to crawl back home. The Father's reception of the son's return is a remarkable message of "grace!" The Father extended forgiveness; He threw a party; He restored his prodigal son to sonship immediately! The elder brother had been working in the field all day. He had been faithful day after day in serving the Father. Upon his arrival and hearing the noise of the party, he was irate. He refused to participate in the joy because it wasn't fair! It made no sense! The prodigal should not be allowed back as a son but as a slave. The party should belong to the brother who had been faithful. But the Father's heart was one of "bleed, suffer, and die" and "never think about yourself." It makes no sense to the demonic spirit.

A thief, a criminal of the worst kind, and a murderer hangs on a cross beside Jesus. In the last moments of his life, he cries, *"Jesus, remember me when You come into Your kingdom"* (Luke 23:42). Immediately, Jesus replied, *"Truly, I say to you, today you will be with Me in paradise"* (Luke 23:43). There is no justice in this response. He does not deserve such an acceptance compared to me. I have worked for the church, given abundant money, and taught a class. Does he get the same gold streets I do? Mine should be thicker than his! Is his mansion going to be as large as mine? He should have a shack on the back forty! That makes no sense to "get, grab, demand, and protect" and "always think about yourself."

We live with the mindset of *"An eye for an eye and a tooth for a tooth"* (Matthew 5:38). There must be justice in the world. Justice is not found in me having one eye, while the one who injured me has two. He should have to pay! Why? Because my spirit is "grab, get, demand, and protect" and "always think about myself."

But I cannot help that I think this way. I cannot keep those thoughts from coming into my heart and mind. They are spontaneous in my life. That is Paul's message to us. We must be *"in Christ."* Only in Jesus do you find "bleed, suffer, and die" and "never think about yourself." "In Jesus," I not only experience the grace of God, but I can become the grace of God extended!

A PURPOSE

If I receive God's grace as Jesus did, will I be exalted and receive *"the name that is above every name"*? Obviously, NO! In a previous study, we discovered Jesus was *"born in the likeness of men"* (Philippians 2:7). Note the word *"men,"* not "man." Jesus did not have my DNA or fingerprints; He had His own. The wonder of *"men"* or humanity is each individual's purpose, design, and destiny. Paul described us as the "body of Christ" (1 Corinthians 12). Each member fulfills the life of the body with a distinct purpose. Jesus has a purpose and ministry that I do not have. My death will not redeem the world, nor will I be King of the Kingdom!

But as Jesus' purpose and destiny is unique, so is mine. As Jesus' purpose and destiny are necessary, so is mine. God did not create me and try to fit me into a plan; God had a plan, and I was born out of the plan of God. God had a dream, and He created me out of His dreams! Do you understand how contrary "get, grab, demand, and protect" and "always think about yourself" is to this reality? Unless Jesus lived in the fullness of God's nature, He would never have fulfilled God's plan. "Bleed, suffer, and die" and "never think about yourself" brought Him to *"not as I will, but as You will"* (Matthew 26:39). The heart of God reaches into my life with gigantic fingers to enhance, fulfill, and establish my life. That movement is coming from the nature of God's heart. It abides in the deep gut level of His being and is a driving force that constantly spills forth with "bleed, suffer, and die" and "never think about yourself" (Philippians 2:1-4). There is an amazing destiny and purpose for my living, but I will never accomplish it without the "spirit of Christmas," the "grace" of God, fully operating in my life. The only blockade to this fulfillment is the demonic spirit!

But if I don't look out for ME, who will? If I don't think about myself, who will? "Always think about myself" has brought nothing but ruin, chaos, and destruction to everything I have touched. Could I "never think about myself," allowing Jesus to be the flowing grace of God to fulfill His purpose for my life?

7

THE NAME

Philippians 2:9-11

"Therefore God has highly exalted Him and bestowed on Him the name that is above every name, so that at the name of Jesus every knee should bow, in heaven and on earth and under the earth, and every tongue confess that Jesus Christ is Lord, to the glory of God the Father" (Philippians 2:9-11).

The name of Jesus is abundantly emphasized in both the Scriptures and the worship experience of the evangelical church. We sing songs focused on the name of Jesus, offer prayers, and conduct spiritual warfare in His name. We are convinced that Jesus' name is essential in the Christmas story. ***"She will bear a Son, and you shall call His name Jesus, for He will save His people from their sins"*** (Matthew 1:21) was the angel's message that convinced Joseph. Every miracle in the early Church declared the name of Jesus (Acts 3:6). The conflict between the early Church and the leaders of Israel focused on His name.

In both court encounters, the Sanhedrin's single demand was that the apostles stop teaching and preaching in the name of Jesus (Acts 4:18; 5:28). Peter clearly articulated the message of the early Church, *"And there is salvation in no one else, for there is no other name under heaven given among men by which we must be saved"* (Acts 4:12).

In the Old Testament, a name is not just a collection of sounds identifying a person, place, or thing. A name expresses the essence of something. The name Esau, meaning "hairy," was quite fitting for the firstborn son of Rebekah and Isaac since what was most noticed about him, physically, was his hairy body (Genesis 25:25). Esau's twin brother, Jacob, came out of the womb gripping Esau's heel. Jacob means "heel-grabber" (Genesis 25:26). This same trait foreshadowed Jacob's adult character, as Jacob later stole the birthright that rightfully belonged to his older brother (Genesis 27:1-45). He tricked his father-in-law, Laban, making Jacob extremely wealthy (Genesis 30:25-43). But in the great wrestling match with God, his name was changed to *"Israel, for you have striven with God and with men, and have prevailed"* (Genesis 32:28).

Jesus is the Greek form of the Hebrew name Joshua, meaning "Savior!" Thus, the name of Jesus declares His mission! Therefore, to know the name of Jesus means to know something about the fundamental traits, nature, and destiny of His person. When you invoke the name, you invoke the Person. The name of Jesus has no significance or power outside of the person of Jesus. His name is not a magical statement we use for personal gain. When we speak the name of Jesus, we acknowledge we are bowing under the authority of His person!

"Therefore God has highly exalted Him and bestowed on Him the name that is above every name" (Philippians 2:9). Let me remind you that Paul makes two statements that explain each other. What does *"God has highly exalted Him"* actually mean? The content is *"bestowed on Him the name that is above every name."* In searching for the meaning of Jesus receiving a superior name, we must grasp *"God has highly exalted Him!"* You must not divide these two statements because Paul intertwined them for understanding. Let us begin with the following understanding!

NOT PRINCIPLE BUT PERSON

There is a Biblical principle that is irrefutable because it is stated repeatedly in both the Old and New Testaments. We must acknowledge its reality, whether discussing Christian theology or pagan practices. The principle is stated in the first four verses of our chapter (Philippians 2:1-4). Paul presents a contrast between the nature of God and the demonic nature. "Bleed, suffer, and die" and "never think about yourself" is radical compared to "get, grab, demand, and protect" and "always think about yourself."

In reading Paul's description of this contrast, the statement becomes an imperative, a command. However, none of the verbs describing or stating the natures are such. The imperative is in Paul's admonishment to *"complete my joy"* (Philippians 2:2). Immediately, this reminds us that the statement of the Biblical principle is not a command or law but an expression of reality. Paul does not propose accomplishing a rule to do but a nature to experience. Such an encouragement specifies what Paul knows or suspects is occurring in the ministry at Philippi. *"Selfish ambition"* is a translation of the Greek word "eritheia" (Philippians 2:3). In the verb form, it is usually in the middle voice, speaking of personal benefit. It has to do with working for hire, which is earning, a motivation of self-interest. Paul was aware that *"some indeed preach Christ from envy and rivalry, but others from good will"* (Philippians 1:15). *"The former proclaim Christ out of self ambition, not sincerely but thinking to afflict me in my imprisonment"* (Philippians 1:17).

In a further description of the demonic nature, Paul uses the term *"conceit"* (Philippians 2:3), a translation of the Greek word "kenodoxian." This word only appears once in the New Testament. It is vainglory, empty pride, and desire for praise that only the self-blessed can lavish on themselves. This word occurs throughout the Greco-Roman world to describe those who think too highly of themselves, not those who might appear to have grounds for "glory," but those whose "glory" is altogether baseless. Paul refers to Euodia and Syntyche as not getting along and encourages all to *"Do all things without grumbling or disputing"* (Philippians 2:14; 4:2). The demonic mindset is destructive to all relationships, especially for the witness to a world filled with the ruin of the demonic nature (Philippians 2:15).

In His final public message, Jesus said, *"Whoever exalts himself will be humbled, and whoever humbles himself will be exalted"* (Matthew 23:12). He said this at the climax of a series of statements describing the self-centered Pharisees. They seek the best seats in the synagogues; they love the titles, labeling them superior to others. They do all of their deeds to be seen by men. They make their phylacteries broad and their fringes long. It is the demonic nature of "grab, get, demand, protect" and "always think about yourself." Jesus makes the same statement at the close of a parable about the Pharisee and the tax collector. While both went to the temple to pray, the Pharisee's prayer was about himself. The Pharisee was unlike the lowly tax collector because he fasted, tithed, and observed the law. The tax collector could not even lift his eyes to heaven but beat his chest in repentance and cried out for mercy because he was a sinner. Jesus said, *"For everyone who exalts himself will be humbled, but the one who humbles himself will be exalted"* (Luke 18:14).

While this is a Biblical principle, Paul does not attempt to establish a pattern of activity or rule for which we should strive. He breaks into what the early Church considered a hymn. It was a celebration of Christ's humiliation concluding in exaltation. This illustration of Jesus verifies the universal law that humiliation will be issued in exaltation, but Paul does not present this illustration for that purpose! This example is not about a principle but about a Person. While Jesus' humility and glory illustrate the principle, He is more excellent than such. He is the principle! The nature of God in Jesus is the principle!

Jesus is God (Philippians 2:6); Jesus is Man (Philippians 2:7). The "bleed, suffer, and die" and "never think about yourself" nature of God drove Jesus to empty Himself of all the advantages of being God (Philippians 2:7). This nature projected Jesus *"to the point of death, even death on a cross"* (Philippians 2:8). The demonic nature of "grab, get, demand, and protect" and "always think about yourself" exerted all of its power to conquer the nature in Jesus. While rejoicing echoed throughout hell, the life of Divine nature exploded into resurrection, ascension, and seating Jesus at the right hand of God! Humiliation became exaltation, which is not merely a principle but a nature in Jesus. A law to master is not Paul's intent, but a nature to experience *"in Christ"* is his cry!

The exaltation of Jesus is not a demonstration of God's power, sovereignty, or omnipotence. Instead, it demonstrates His nature. Jesus did not view His suffering as necessary to earn, merit, or deserve the exaltation. Jesus did not accomplish the cross to get; such an attitude would violate the nature possessing Him. Becoming man could not get Him what He already has; He is God! Jesus already possessed the highest position in being God! In the nature of God, "bleed, suffer, and die" and "never think about yourself," there can be no selfish element present. Any intent to "get, grab, demand, or protect" and "always think about yourself" creates a mixture that cannot exist!

Paul declares, ***"He humbled Himself by becoming obedient to the point of death, even the death on the cross"*** (Philippians 2:8). Jesus did not surrender to death on the cross to receive the reward of exaltation. Paul clearly said that Jesus emptied Himself, served, and died without a promise of reward. As a Man, Jesus embraced the cross as His obedient service came to a bitter end. In our passage, ***"becoming"*** is a translation of the Greek word "ginomai." It means "beginning, birthing, coming into existence, beginning to be." This word is a circumstantial participle, a verb having both the characteristics of a verb and an adjective. In this case, it expresses the conditions or circumstances in which death occurs. The Greek word "hypekoos" is translated as *"obedient"* and is a predicate adjective proposing that *"He humbled Himself"* is equal to *"becoming obedient to the point of death, even the death on the cross."* The extraordinary fact is that Christ died as an act of obedience without a promise of reward. On the cross, Christ's future was closed. Jesus' grave was a cave, not a tunnel. There was no view of gain! That is precisely what the Trinity God exalted. He vindicated "bleed, suffer, and die" and "never think about yourself" with no claim of return, no eye upon a reward.

This reality is within the Person of Jesus! It is the nature of the fullness of the Spirit of Jesus (Philippians 2:1). This is Paul's appeal to us. *"Have this mind among yourselves, which is yours in Christ Jesus"* (Philippians 2:5). "Get, grab, demand, and protect" and "always think about yourself" have always dominated our lives. Would we not automatically approach religion with the same intent? What will be my reward? How will I benefit? What will God do for me? While most religions will tolerate such an approach, Christianity will not! We are to merge with the nature of Jesus. The moment any intent of gain or reward emerges, it violates God's heart. Christ calls us to crucifixion with Him. Will we merge with His nature? Will we abandon ourselves to Him? Will we be obedient without the expectation of reward?

NOT POSITIONAL BUT PREPOSTEROUS

The explanatory statement of Jesus' exaltation continues with *"above every name"* (Philippians 2:9). It is a prepositional phrase beginning with the preposition *"above,"* translated from the Greek word "hyper." None of the New Testament writers used this Greek word, like the apostle Paul. He used it by itself and consistently linked it with other Greek words, creating compound words. In this case, Paul used it to introduce a prepositional phrase. The preposition is *"above,"* translated from "hyper," and the accusative or direct object is *"name,"* translated from "onoma." Whenever "hyper" is used in this grammar structure, it expresses an intensification.

For example, Jesus said, *"Whoever loves father or mother more* (hyper) *than Me is not worthy of Me, and whoever loves son or daughter more* (hyper) *than Me is not worthy of Me"* (Matthew 10:37). Paul used this grammar structure in his testimony. *"And I was advancing in Judaism beyond* (hyper) *many of my own age"* (Galatians 1:14). There are numerous examples of the use of this Greek word to express intensity. Regarding the believer, Paul cried, *"No, in all things we are more* (hyper) *than conquerors through Him who loved us"* (Romans 8:37). In this case, Paul linked "hyper" with another Greek word, "nikao." This Greek compound word is the excessive, preposterous statement found in the conquering lifestyle of the believer in Christ. No one would look at these statements and propose a "position." The emphasis of the Greek word "hyper" in each case is the "greatest, highest, excessive, extravagant" manner of the condition.

The extravagant use of "hyper" is true in our passage! The name given to Jesus is abundantly, excessively beyond any other name. The name of Jesus is not inserted into a position He occupies but embraces Him for the Person He is! Remember, there are two statements in our passage explaining each other. ***"Therefore God has highly exalted Him"*** (Philippians 2:9). What does this mean? Has the Trinity God given Jesus a throne upon which to sit? Has He placed titles before and credentials after His name? Has the Trinity God made Jesus "boss" or "supervisor?" This same question carries over into the two following verses, ***"so that at the name of Jesus every knee should bow, in heaven and on earth and under the earth, and every tongue confess that Jesus Christ is Lord, to the glory of God the Father"*** (Philippians 2:10, 11). Is His title ***"Lord?"*** Is that a position?

Paul's emphasis is not positional but describes the excessive abundance happening within Jesus through His relationship with the Trinity God within His humanity. The Trinity God exalts Jesus to the highest possible degree in the relationship a human being can have with God. Jesus fulfills the Trinity God's dream in His creation of humanity. It is not a title before His name or a certificate of achievement on His office wall. The exaltation is in who Jesus has become through the fullness of the Spirit of God!

In one of our early pastorates, an elderly church member was a retired school teacher. "Miss Willie" had never been married but, through the years, had mothered the entire neighborhood. The presence of Jesus so permeated her life that sweetness, kindness, and constant encouragement filled the atmosphere around her. Those desiring spiritual growth wanted to be in her presence, hoping they could absorb what she was into them. She had no position in the church, no title or authority. She had not acquired a position of authority; she had become a "saint!"

Jesus has not achieved His long-time dream of being ***"Lord"*** over us. He did not finally receive the promotion

He worked so hard to earn. In His helplessness, being one with us, Jesus abandoned Himself to the depth of humiliation, *"to the point of death, even the death of a cross."* Did He not submit Himself entirely to sin's total penalty and consequence and become cursed by God? Was He not encompassed by the absolute ruin and damnation of sin, hell? Was He not helpless in the face of such humiliation? BUT the total embracing of His helplessness allowed the Trinity God to exalt Him, not to a position but to a relationship.

I hesitated to use the word "preposterous" as a part of the title for this truth. But is it not true? It is unbelievable, unreasonable, unthinkable, and indeed preposterous that a human being like us could go from the depths of sin to the fullness of all God's dreams for humanity. Yet, Jesus, the Man, has been granted by grace this intimacy with God. The nature of God, "bleed, suffer, and die," and "never think about yourself," is fully possessing a Man. Jesus is the total expression of God's heart.

"Have this mind among yourselves, which is yours in Christ Jesus" (Philippians 2:5). That is the cry of Paul for our lives. The excessive, preposterous reality of oneness with the nature of God that Jesus experienced is now ours in Him! Has He not paved a highway from the lowest of hell to the height of oneness with God's heart? Can I not know the love of the Father as Jesus does (John 17:23)? Am I not His brother (Hebrews 2:11)? Are we not *"children of God, and if children, then heirs - heirs of God and fellow heirs with Christ"* (Romans 8:16-17)? Jesus embraced my helplessness so I could embrace His exaltation!

8

TO THE GLORY

Philippians 2:10-11

"So that at the name of Jesus every knee should bow, in heaven and on earth and under the earth, and every tongue confess that Jesus Christ is Lord, to the glory of God the Father" (Philippians 2:10-11).

Verses 10 and 11 grammatically depend upon the key revelation of the previous verse (Philippians 2:9). Jesus is *"highly exalted"* by God. This exaltation is evident in that God *"bestowed on Him the name that is above every name."* The first Greek word in the text is "hina," in order that! As stated in these two verses, the exaltation of Jesus by the Trinity God is for a distinct purpose. The grace of God highlighted in the declaration of *"bestowed on Him"* establishes the foundation of the exaltation. The Greek word "charizomai" is the verb form of "charis," translated as "grace." It is by the unmerited, not earned "bleed, suffer, die" and "never think about yourself" nature of God that exalts Jesus!

One might attempt to make a case for Jesus' worthiness being in His *"becoming obedient to the point of death, even the death on a cross"* (Philippians 2:9). Certainly, the Book of Revelation is filled with references to *"Worthy is the Lamb who was slain"* (Revelation 5:12). Has His obedience made Him worthy? Recognize the reality of Jesus becoming a helpless man without spiritual resources. The truth that Jesus, as a Man, had a choice is a result of "prevenient grace!" How does anyone know the truth, feel the compulsion of truth, and respond to truth? It is by the grace of God! How could anyone take credit for obedience when the act of obeying flows from the grace of God? Worthiness if not in earning, but in "grace!" The "grace nature" of God exalted Jesus! Overshadowing these two statements is the hymn formation of the phrases found in the early Church. All Biblical scholars agree that the believers repeated these statements often in their worship experience. They were the typical expression of their view of Jesus. However, it must be understood these phrases were proposed nearly 800 years before their pronouncement in the early Church. God spoke through the prophet Isaiah:

> *"To Me every knee shall bow, every tongue shall swear allegiance" (Isaiah 45:23).*

These words are in a lengthy poetic statement beginning with the phrase,

> *"Thus says the Lord" (Isaiah 45:14).*

Within this poetic statement, *"the Lord"* is a translation

of the Hebrew word "YHWH," which is "Yahweh." The Old Testament writers consistently translated it as *"the Lord,"* representing the name the God of Israel gave to the Israelites through Moses concerning Himself. In the Septuagint, *"Lord"* appears over nine thousand times; in over six thousand passages, *"Lord"* replaces Yahweh, Jehovah. By New Testament times, *"Lord"* was so highly esteemed it was rarely spoken out loud.

The context of Yahweh's *"the Lord"* statement in Isaiah contains the creation of the heavens, the earth, and all its inhabitants (Isaiah 45:18). He did not hide from that inhabitance. Still, He requested they seek Him for His revelation (Isaiah 45:19). Some foolishly carry man-made idols who cannot save, for there is no other god besides Him (Isaiah 45:20-21). God pleads with them,

"Turn to me and be saved, all the ends of the earth! For I am God, and there is no other" (Isaiah 45:22).

"The Lord," the only God, Yahweh, Jehovah is the One who says,

"To Me every knee shall bow, every tongue shall swear allegiance" (Isaiah 45:23).

Believers declare Yahweh to be God alone, over all creation, and thus over all other gods and nations. He is Israel's Savior, whom they can fully trust. Indeed, He offers salvation to everyone but declares that *"to Me every knee shall bow"* in respect and recognition of who He is!

Do you see Paul's declaration? We have come full circle! He began with the bold proclamation of the Divinity of

Jesus (Philippians 2:6). Jesus is God! He is the objective reality of God; everything true about God is true about Jesus. He is Yahweh, Jehovah! But Jesus became Man, the objective reality of humanity (Philippians 2:7). To do so, He *"emptied Himself"* of every aspect of Divine possessions that was not compatible with being human (Philippians 2:7). But He did not just become human, but became a human *"servant"* (Philippians 2:7). In fact, He pushed this sacrifice to the limits *"to the point of death, even the death on a cross"* (Philippians 2:8).

But this "bleed, suffer, die" and "never think about yourself" nature of the Trinity God exalted Him by grace! The content of the exaltation is in the grace-filled gift of *"the name"* (Philippians 2:11). It is *"the name that is above every name"* (Philippians 2:10). At this name *"every knee should bow, in heaven and on earth and under the earth"* (Philippians 2:10). In fact, *"every tongue confess that Jesus Christ is Lord, to the glory of God the Father"* (Philippians 2:11). BUT, wait! Yahweh, Jehovah, the Trinity God, said that it would only be *"to Me"* that such bowing and confessing would occur! How is Jesus, the Man, receiving such recognition? It is because He is God! But Jesus is Man! He is the God-Man! The Trinity God recognizes Him as the objective reality of God and exalts Him with the declaration of *"Lord!"* The Trinity God is embracing Him as God! Did Jesus give up being a Man? NO! He did not fill Himself with all He had *"emptied Himself!"* The Trinity God recognizes Jesus as God with His attachment to humanity! Listen to these verses.

"God has made Him both Lord and Christ, this Jesus whom you crucified" (Acts 2:36).

"Therefore I want you to understand that no one speaking in the Spirit of God ever says 'Jesus is accursed!' and no one can say 'Jesus is Lord' except in the Holy Spirit" (1 Corinthians 12:3).

"If you confess with your mouth that Jesus is Lord and believe in your heart that God raised Him from the dead, you will be saved" (Romans 10:9).

"But we believe that we will be saved through the grace of the Lord Jesus, just as they will" (Acts 15:11).

ROADWAY

What does this mean? Everyone is recognizing Jesus as Divine! He is God, and everyone will proclaim Him as such! *"Every knee should bow, in heaven and on earth and under the earth"* (Philippians 2:10). The whole created order shall give Jesus respect as God. *"Every knee should bow"* is a common idiom for doing homage. It is always in recognition of the authority of the god or person to whom one is offering such respect. The full scope of this recognition is in those *"in heaven and on earth and under the earth,"* giving recognition to the fact Jesus is God! Those *"in heaven"* refer to all the heavenly beings, angels, and demons. Those *"on earth"* refer to all those living on earth at the time of the declaration. Those *"under the earth"* may refer to those who have died and will be raised to participate in this declaration (John 5:28-29).

Many Biblical scholars relate the activity of these two verses to the second coming of Christ. Logic would indicate that every knee bowing and every tongue confessing has not occurred in this present moment, suggesting there is a completion to this recognition by the Trinity God that is yet to come. *"Highly exalted,"* *"bestowed,"* *"should bow,"* and *"confess"* are all in the aorist tense. We do not have any tense in the English language comparable to it. It entirely focuses on the verb's action, not the time of its occurrence. I could not find one passage referring to this exaltation that is not in the aorist tense. However, if the verb is in the aorist tense and the indicative mood (a simple statement of fact), the aorist usually denotes past time. That is the case with *"highly exalted"* and *"bestowed"* but not *"should bow"* and *"confess."* Therefore, we would conclude that Jesus is exalted and recognized as God in the exaltation in the past, but His entire creation does not acknowledge the full wonder of this at this time.

The startling issue of Paul's statement is his substituting *"at the name of Jesus"* for what God said through Isaiah, *"to Me!"* Several times throughout the Isaiah passage God declared, *"I am the Lord, and there is no other"* (Isaiah 45:18). *"And there is no other god besides Me, a righteous God and a Savior; there is none besides Me"* (Isaiah 45:21). *"For I am God, and there is no other"* (Isaiah 45:22). Then, this God states, *"To Me every knee shall bow, every tongue shall swear allegiance"* (Isaiah 45:23). Now Paul changes the statement to *"at the name of Jesus"* (Philippians 2:10). All that Yahweh, Jehovah, the Trinity God said about Himself now applies to Jesus! All the respect, worship, and recognition as creator and God over all other gods and nations we now see as given to Jesus, who is *"Lord,"* Yahweh."

But Jesus is Man! Is this not the wonder of this startling truth? God who *"emptied Himself"* of all He had as God, without giving up being God, and became Man, is embraced again by the Trinity God as God! Perhaps this speaks directly to the reality of His cry, *"My God, My God, why have You forsaken Me"* (Matthew 27:46)? Yahweh could not embrace a Man who assumed the entire sin of the human race within Himself as if it were His own. Such a Man must know the total destructive power and ruin of "grab, get, demand, protect" and "always think about yourself," the demonic nature. Would God not need to reject such a Man? Indeed, is it not a great mystery? In conquering sin and hell, God exalted this Man; He is *"Lord,"* and His position as God is again recognized! But He is a Man! He is my brother! I am joint-heir with Him! He is a Man who has created a direct avenue to the heart of God. All the nature of God, "bleed, suffer, die" and "never think about yourself," flows through this Man. He has brought me into the same nature of God! With one arm firmly embracing God, for *"Jesus is Lord,"* and one arm firmly embracing man, for Jesus is Man, He brings God and man into a new relationship. All Jesus is as a man He extends to me! I can be like Him, Christlikeness!

REASON

Paul quickly adds the excellent purpose for such a declaration by the Trinity God. It is *"to the glory of God the Father"* (Philippians 2:11). The Trinity God recognizes the Divine nature of Jesus for His glory! The word *"to"* is critical in understanding the statement's impact. It is a translation of the Greek word "eis," a moving term in contrast with "in," which is fixed. It bespeaks motion into anything, and its use as a preposition of purpose expresses the purpose for which the related verbal action occurs. The Divinity of Jesus is recognized and proclaimed by the Trinity God by *"highly exalted Him and bestowing on Him the name"* (Philippians 2:9). This name is excessively beyond the recognition of any other name since it is this *"Lord"* before whom all will bow and all will confess (Philippians 2:10, 11). Therefore, this exaltation moves us into *"the glory of God the Father."* Accordingly, the purpose of the exaltation is not a self-centered desire of the Trinity God to receive praise but to highlight the Divine nature in Jesus, which would draw us to desire to be like Him! God has already planted within us a hunger for His nature. Now, God excessively proclaims His nature, drawing everyone to it.

The purpose of the exaltation is that we might experience the *"glory"* belonging only to Yahweh, Jehovah, our God! *"Glory"* is a translation of the Greek word "doxa." The root word of "doxa" is "dokeo," meaning "to think or suppose." As the word developed in Greek culture, it evolved into "doxa," primarily meaning "thought or opinion." It focused mainly on favorable human opinion and, thus, in a secondary sense, focused on reputation, praise, honor, splendor, light, and perfection. Applying "doxa" to man reflects human opinion and is shifty, uncertain, and often based on error. The *"glory"* of man reflects the demonic nature man has adopted. His entire perspective flows from the nature of "get, grab, demand, protect" and "always think about yourself."

During the wilderness temptation of Jesus, the devil took Him to a very high mountain and showed *"all the kingdoms of the world and their glory* (doxa)*"* (Matthew 4:8). The devil promised Jesus all of these kingdoms if He would simply fall down and worship him (Matthew 4:8). Jesus refused because He had no desire to possess kingdoms that had the perspective, the opinion, or the nature of the devil. These kingdoms all had the *"glory"* or "doxa" of the demonic nature, "get, grab, demand, protect" and "always think about yourself." These kingdoms experienced the ruin and destruction of this nature, *"glory."* This "doxa" was repulsive to the Divine nature of "bleed, suffer, die" and "never think about yourself." It is a different *"glory."*

The glory of God is one of *"encouragement"* (Philippians 2:1), desiring to prosper, build, and enhance. This *"glory"* forms gigantic fingers to reach into the lives of others to establish them, not ruin them. This *"glory"* is the nature of God, *"the comfort from love"* (Philippians 2:1), the resource of the moving nature of God. The chief characteristic of such a resource is *"affection"* concerning bowels, at the gut level of all that God is in His core being. This *"glory"* of God is faithful and changeless, marking the actual value of things as they appear to the eternal mind.

In speaking with the Pharisees concerning the *"glory"* they received among themselves, Jesus corrected them on their focus. They readily affirmed each other in their selfish perspectives because they focused on each other's opinions. They did not *"seek the glory* (doxa) *that comes from the only God"* (John 5:44). The nature of God, "bleed, suffer, die," and "never think about yourself" was not what they pursued. *"For they loved the glory that comes from man more than the glory that comes from God"* (John 12:43). The *"glory"* of God is His unchanging essence, His nature. Jesus is the expression of this *"glory,"* "bleed, suffer, die," and "never think about yourself!" This nature exalts and recognizes Him as God; Jesus is exalted as a Man and identified with God's nature. He established through His life, death, and exaltation a road to the heart of God. In Him, I can experience the nature of God. I become the *"glory of God the Father"* as Jesus was!

Paul brings us back to His imperative, *"complete my joy by being of the same mind"* (Philippians 2:2). There was conflict within the Philippi church (Philippians 1:15; 4:2). The cause of contention was the demonic nature. It always brings destruction and ruin. We must be *"in Christ."* Here, we find the Divine nature, "bleed, suffer, die" and "never think about yourself." As it was with Jesus, we cannot earn or merit it. No amount of obedience will deserve it. Jesus must fill us with Himself. If the Divine nature is gifted to us *"in Christ,"* it will cleanse and crucify the demonic nature. We must merge with Jesus until we think like Him, feel like Him, and want what He desires! Outside of Christ, this is impossible. "Christ in us" is the call!

www.ingramcontent.com/pod-product-compliance
Lightning Source LLC
Chambersburg PA
CBHW061153040426
42445CB00013B/1668